Advance praise for Hawk Madrone's

Weeding at Dawn

"Hawk Madrone has chronicled a difficult yet rewarding way of life in an appealing manner. . . . In *Weeding at Dawn*, this Mary Daly of the woods shares with the reader the sense of peace she has found while living . . . by her principles in a place of serenity. The writer goes beyond journaling to autobiography and a slice of lesbian herstory."

–Lee Lynch, author of *Cactus Love*, the *Morton River Valley Trilogy*, and *The Swashbuckler*; syndicated columnist and social worker

"A richly descriptive and achingly honest portrait of the physical and emotional labor required to homestead in the country, *Weeding at Dawn* maps the feel and intimacy of a personal journey. . . . Readers will find in Madrone's work the thoughtful, close observations of nature and the resulting philosophical ruminations of our very own lesbian Thoreau."

–Kay Turner, author of *Beautiful Necessity: The Art and Meaning of Women's Altars*

"[Madrone's] evocative, sometimes haunting memories, which range from the youthful eagerness of the women's back-to-the-land movement of the 1970s to the musings of a woman growing older as a new century dawns, offer an unusual vantage point on three decades of lesbian history-in-the-making."

–Peggy Pascoe, Beekman Chair of Northwest and Pacific History, University of Oregon

WEEDING AT DAWN:
A LESBIAN COUNTRY LIFE

Alice Street Editions

Past Perfect, by Judith P. Stelboum

Inside Out, by Juliet Carrera

Façades, by Alex Marcoux

Weeding at Dawn: A Lesbian Country Life, by Hawk Madrone

Forthcoming

His Hands, His Tools, His Sex, His Dress: Lesbian Writers on Their Fathers, edited by Catherine Reid and Holly K. Iglesias

Yin Fire, by Alexandra Grilikhes

Treat, by Angie Vicars

Extraordinary Couples, Ordinary Lives, by Lynn Haley-Banez and Joanne Garrett

WEEDING AT DAWN:
A LESBIAN COUNTRY LIFE

Hawk Madrone

Alice Street Editions

Harrington Park Press

New York • London • Oxford

Published by

Alice Street Editions, Harrington Park Press®, an imprint of The Haworth Press, Inc., 10 Alice Street, Binghamton, NY 13904-1580 USA (www.HaworthPress.com).

Cover photograph by Hawk Madrone.
Cover design by Thomas J. Mayshock Jr.

Library of Congress Cataloging-in-Publication Data

Madrone, Hawk.
     Weeding at dawn : a lesbian country life / Hawk Madrone.
        p. cm.
     ISBN 1-56023-206-4 (alk. paper)–ISBN 1-56023-207-2 (pbk. : alk. paper)
     1. Madrone, Hawk. 2. Rural lesbians–Oregon–Biography. I. Title.
HQ75.4.M324 A3 2000
305.48'9664'0979529–dc21
[B]
                                        00-033142

This Book
Is
Dedicated to

Caius
Lavy
Phyrste
Missy Moonshine
Ladydog
Moongoose
Mailava
Sami Slate
Lillith One
Keaton
Cave Kidden
and Muphin,
steadfast companions, all.

CONTENTS

Preface

In 1960, the graduate class in Eastern Philosophy was a far reach for me, an auditing junior, but the professor had a reputation that pulled me beyond my limitations, at least for a few classes. I didn't really understand many of the concepts, but the *sense* of what a Hindu thinker might ponder was borne by the lectures delivered in a slow, almost chanting cadence that painted pictures, called up spirit. One day, to communicate a particularly difficult point, he droned a story of a Red-tailed hawk gliding . . . gliding between high ridges, riding the currents of wind over a long valley, graceful and free.

Soon into the semester my full load of for-credit classes was as much as I could handle, and I stopped going to those mesmerizing lectures. But the hawk stayed with me. Years later, on the opposite end of the continent, living in a cabin in the forest with my lover, I wanted a new name, a way to call my spirit, a way for Susan to speak to the wisest and deepest part of me. I recalled the image of the Red-tailed hawk, and I became her, graceful and free.

For ten years I was called Hawk, even after I had moved again, several times, even after Susan and I had parted and my woman-loving life had taken on, and lost, new faces. In those years I had come home to this isolated hilltop in southern Oregon, where I continue to live. Here I gaze at a wide expanse of sky, study the distant ridges, and sometimes envy a hawk's aerobatics. But it was the trees of this land who tugged at my naming, and teased me with change, with refocus. Here I plant myself in the solidity and sureness of soil; here I walk among the madrones, whose bodies glisten in the rain, whose branches twine like a woman's muscular arm, who drop their old leaves every Summer, but are evergreen, whose small white bell-shaped blooms sweeten the Spring air, and give way to tiny red fruit. A versatile tree, the madrone, and tenacious: on the government land at our northern boundary, the madrones were incised, to kill them slowly and make way for the growing marketable conifers. Shortly after I moved here, I walked among the standing skeletons of trees, and was amazed to find a few who had knit their wounds and still flexed their branches in the sun.

Madrone became my second name, as it was my second nature.

With time, the madrones pulled me to the sound of their name, and I began being called by the second half of my name, Madrone.

The stories and poems in this book appear in the order in which they were written – sometimes originally in my journal – over a span of a little more than two decades of my life on this land. Some were originally written in the present tense, and are published here as such, though the surrounding material places them in their respective niches of time. While each "chapter" bears its own internal integrity, their progression forms a history, an unfolding of my self.

Madrone

Acknowledgments

For the past dozen years or so, I have been sharing my work with The Southern Oregon Women Writers' Group, Gourmet Eating Society (we have great potlucks), and Chorus (sometimes one of us writes a song, and of course we all must learn it). Every third Sunday I am blessed with the supportive and helpfully critical listening of friends, as well as by the inspiration of their writing. I am indebted to them for their encouragement and praise, which has kept me aimed toward this wider sharing of the details and spirit of my life. I am particularly grateful to: Mab Maher for her sense of what gives deeper meaning to the work; Tee Corinne who kept nudging and believing; Bethroot Gwynn for her sharp eye for better phrasing; Tangren Alexander whose oohs and ahs and example kept me writing more.

I am thankful as well to Judith Barrington of *The Flight of the Mind* Writing Workshops for Women, who said just the right things about my writing to help me stay convinced it was definitely worth doing; Gayl Bowser, who began all this with her computer, typing my early stories, then helping me learn to do it myself, and continuing to support my writing in many ways; Lesbian Natural Resources, for the grant that made getting a computer possible; Francis Eatherington, whose generosity and computer expertise have been a balm; Jeanne Davies and Helen Laurence, who critiqued the manuscript and made excellent suggestions for final revisions; Helen Mallon, Romilda Crocamo, Julie Ehlers, all of The Harrington Park/ Haworth Press, whose loving work with my manuscript was this writer's dream come true; and most especially to every woman who has come to me after public readings, or after reading something I've had published, and told me she was moved, pleased, satisfied. It is for all these women, after my own pleasure, that I write.

A gray day in January. The cold rains of the southern Oregon Winter give me permission to stay indoors after I have fed the hens. Tending the woodstove, the cats, my dog companion Muphin, and myself, are my only really necessary chores, so I can sit at my desk and reflect, remember . . . when there was no desk, not even a house, back over twenty-one years ago when this land, this life, were still only a vision.

Fly Away Home

In early 1975 a woman disbursed a large friendly divorce settlement among several of her friends – "so that women might love themselves." Bethroot, my new lover, was one of the recipients. We each were swept up in the dyke back-to-the-land movement of the 1970s, encouraged by friends who had already moved to the hills of southern Oregon. We wanted to join the tribe, the wide network of Lesbians who were rooting their spirituality in the soil, the cycles of the earth, intent upon separating ourselves as much as possible from the world the men have made. Because of the gift, there was money for a downpayment, and we wanted land. So we started looking that Summer, travelling the circuit of realtors in southwest Oregon, always meeting with the same barren market. We wanted a sanctuary: no less than twenty acres, seclusion, magnificent views, good water, some forest and some open areas, a southern exposure, and preferably some structure adequate for living in, but not a large addition to the cost of the land. Most realtors quickly recognized what we wanted, told us about the long lists they had of others looking for the same paradise. "If you'd come asking around five years ago," they intoned, "there might have been something to show you."

The price of land in these parts had skyrocketed in those five years, and there was less and less available, unless you were very wealthy and looking for parcels of over a hundred acres. We heard realtor after realtor describe the earth, the trees, as commodities, the land an investment. They gave us information about large properties for sale, and pressed on about resale value, subdividing for profit, potential timber harvests. We concentrated on our ideals and listened to the pulse of the earth, as we sometimes together, most often separately, camped out in state parks or at various friends' country homes.

Despite their alien perspective, those realtors were helpful to us as we picked their brains for information about county codes, septic systems, road building, types of buying procedures, easements, taxes, zoning categories, and much more that we knew nothing about when we started on our quest.

We were looking for a home we knew was already there, waiting for us: land sacred to ancient women, to be restored to our women's culture as a place of safety and peace. I especially needed a place isolated from the fast track, where relative silence and solitude might soothe my overly sensitive ears, and simplicity and work with my hands would balance me after years of cities and academia. I needed, too, a home where I could immerse myself in present tasks and invest in a future without Susan, my ex-lover, with whom I had thought I shared a life-time commitment and the intention of settling in the country together. She had gone off just the year before into a new romantic sunset, with Bethroot's best friend; I was still nursing that festering wound, and longed for a home of my own and hard work to do, as a way to healing and happiness.

Bethroot, being more a romantic about country life, was not so motivated as I by the image of trading in head-work for muscle-work, but we pursued our joint vision of womensland with the conviction of true believers.

After three months of near-constant searching, Bethroot moved with her little dog, Lavy, and my German Shepherd, Caius, to a motel manager's job at the coast. I travelled around in my Datsun pickup with Phyrste, a small, mixed version of a Black Lab, who had five years before chosen me with a puppy's pleading in a pet shop window back in my San Francisco days. He and I visited several women's lands, a gypsy life that was to continue for longer than I'd hoped, and I continued with the "realtor work" through much of Autumn and into Winter. When Bethroot had some days off at the motel, we met to search together, determined to find our dream.

Once we thought we found the place we wanted: forty isolated acres bordered by peopleless forests, some owned by a paper company, some by a private investor. The price was right, the land was lovely and we pursued her mightily, though there were serious easement problems as well as a costly bridge and road to be built through neighboring property adjacent to the county road. There were no buildings, indeed no development at all. Some gray mossy boards were all that remained to suggest someone had home-steaded there a few generations before. We would have to start from scratch: find a spring and tap it, or have a well drilled, build our house and outbuildings, beg a garden from the untamed soil, learning how to do most everything as we went.

That land was a winsome test: we had made so many trips, looked so long, and this was the first place we had seen that came anywhere close to what we wanted. We blessed her with our women's circle songs and hooted to the hills there, whose answers were inviting but shy. We did research at the county courthouse, we wooed those at-first hostile neighbors, we tried to estimate the cost of the road and bridge to see if we could possibly afford it. All this was done under tremendous pressure as the seller would not enter an earnest money agreement and said he had another buyer on the line.

Bethroot and I were cautioned by the enormity of this undertak-ing. Our relationship, at a brief honeymoon's end, was already strained. The fact that just the two of us were looking for land together was in itself an unexpected deviation from our original assumptions about who we were together. Susan's and her new lover's departure had left us holding the idea of making a life on the land, and it had taken a lot of pushing and pulling in each of us, as well as between us, to decide to embark on this adventure. We had not exactly seen ourselves as a pioneer couple homestead-ing in the wilderness! While we shared a passion for living close to nature as well as a sense of spiritual mission, and banked on our bottom-line caring for each other to outlast current tensions, we had doubts about our ability to handle all this land would ask of us . . . and they would not go away, so finally we let her go.

The months of visits to realtors and small-town bulletin boards continued. I worried a lot, as was my wont, and was shocked and saddened by the sudden death of Caius, my dog-friend of over seven years. Sometimes I despaired, lost touch with my belief in my ability to manifest what I truly wanted. Bethroot appeared to falter less: "We will find beautiful land," she would nudge through my occasional gloom, quickening both our hopes again. Following our circle-sister Seaweed's suggestion, if we were awake at dawn we meditated on womensland at that hour, connecting with other Lesbians in Oregon and California who were doing the same.

Came March and some more leads to follow, including another forty-acre lot which sounded too expensive, with a road impassable except for the driest months, yet appealing. Bethroot was especially excited and hopeful the day we went to see it, because she had seen a fragment of a rainbow on the sea horizon at dawn. Risa, the realtor I'd met at The Fall Gathering, an annual southern Oregon women's festival, drove us from the little town of Myrtle Creek, which edged the Interstate, out the county road to nearly its end. Then we three, and Lavy and Phyrste, hiked for just over a mile up an old dirt road, with foot-deep ruts, through a beautiful forest, the only sounds birdsong and the mountain air in the trees. The way was steep in lots of places, but as I remember it, my body smiled with each step. Just after crossing the property line, we passed a cabin-size storage building Risa said was called the "gatehouse," then came out to a clearing and saw a hill basking in the almost-Spring sun, stately madrones teasing in the breeze.

It did not take long, not long at all, to sense peace here, to know we had come home. It was the day before my 37th birthday, so I felt incredibly gifted as we walked a little of the forty acres that day, drinking her in, seeing her more obvious charms, even looking for possible flaws. We found complete seclusion, with magnificent 200° hilltop views, and a variety of open areas surrounded by a predominantly evergreen forest. The southern slope of the hill boasted a large fenced garden, and, below that, a small apple orchard, overlooked by a rustic old pole barn (in need of restoration). The other buildings included an unfinished and not yet inhabitable large, round, twelve-sided house, a sweet privy, and a rustic henhouse (complete with a small flock of hens). A cozy propane-run old twenty-foot travel trailer was the available living quarters. Water gushed from an outdoor faucet into a metal drum, running with gravity through a mile-long pipe fed by a mountain spring. All-in-all a slice of heaven indeed.

We did have concern about the potential noise on the well-maintained Bureau of Land Management road which could be seen from one knoll, and, as the land was surrounded by BLM forest on three sides and privately owned timbered hills on the fourth, we knew there would be the sounds and effects of logging in our lives eventually. Weighing this against the sound of close-by neighbors, we opted for the unoccupied forest and the isolation of BLM country. Risa drew up the papers for an offer from us.

Next day, visiting Elizabeth and Elana at Golden, their land one county to the south, we had a fine Pisces party which I enjoyed despite the face-full of poison oak I got from following that water pipe into the forest. Elizabeth gave me a headband she had made with the tail and claws of a Red-tailed hawk, and Bethroot surprised me with a mask she had fashioned from leather, feathers, shells, and bone. The day after that, a Friday, we took some countrydyke friends from nearby Cabbage Lane to see this land we had discovered, all of us excited to bring it into our Lesbian community. We stopped at Risa's office, learned our offer had been rejected, and drew up another which was closer to what the seller, Susan, a young woman in the process of a marriage ending, wanted. Risa, who was her friend, was certain this new offer would buy the place for us.

We spent the weekend with friends at the Fishpond, womensland south and east of Golden, where there was joy all around as we were kidded about "buyer's regrets." I got hardly any sleep: we had just done it at last! I was on my way home, and my mind played with the fantasies of my new life. Then, upon contacting the realtor for the seller's formal answer, we learned it was negative: she had decided not to sell. She realized she could not part with this land she loved so much, though there was a note in it all that said some other time. In months? Years? We didn't know; we were shocked, deflated. I could not believe I could be so sure about this land and then have it become unavailable. None of the guides to property-buying we had studied, or advice from all those realtors, had prepared us for this. We had followed all the proper procedures: found and investigated the place we wanted, made an offer we thought had bought the place for us, but didn't get it! She decided not to sell? Huh? I felt powerless, and yet I was still certain this was the right land.

Well, having no other choice, Phyrste and I continued our life of visiting a week or two here, a week or two there, and Bethroot went back to her temporary home and job by the sea. While it is true my wandering-life was strengthening and inspiring for me in many ways, it was beginning to wear me out, what with hopes of being settled by Summer and here Spring was in bloom. We were going to have to start all over again, look in probably yet a different area, cultivate a new crop of realtors. I was exhausted with all that, and, as I had been doing much of the initial contact with realtors, Bethroot agreed to take over that job. I decided I had to explore other types of energies which I could put to use in this search.

In the following weeks that not-for-sale hilltop stayed in my mind. Each morning as I did yoga I would conjure her, walk among her trees and under the open sky, hear the water running continuously in the drum. That land beckoned me as a lover, and my spirit courted her with great devotion. I opened myself to her entreaty and my mind filled with the images of a small family farm, a gathering place for occasional women's spiritual/cultural events. I imagined a life of daily work with the land and animals, fused with spiritual discipline and celebration. I saw a place where women would visit to experience the spiritual-as-practical, the practical-as-spiritual, where spading the garden and singing in circles were both sacred events. Some friends cautioned me to let go, but I was a woman possessed. I kept my visions clear; the psychic work gave me new strength, and I felt my power rekindled. With Risa's OK, and when I knew no one was home for me to disturb, I visited the land again, and twice drove up the BLM road from where I sang and hooted to her across the draw, the resident rooster crowing in answer.

About mid-April I went to visit Bethroot, taking with me an aerial photograph of the land I had obtained at the county surveyor's office. When I hung it on her living room wall we discovered the form created by the open and forested spaces was that of a dancing woman! Aha! The beckoning spirit even had shape! Each day Bethroot did Tai Chi in that room and my morning meditations continued. Now I soared above the land, guided by the photograph which showed a high-flying hawk's view of the hill.

Our friends Greenbo, Seagull, and LaRosa joined us at the coast to celebrate the growing Spring, and one evening we had our circle. . . . We all dressed in fine costumes (I in my headband and mask) and brought objects special to us to the candlelit center. We passed the rattle and sang many songs about womensland and our lives as countrywomen. We sang loving energy to the woman from whom OWL Farm was purchased and to the women who would live there, the woman realtor through whom Rainbow's End was purchased, and the woman realtor who introduced us to this magical land with the dancing woman. We sang loving energy to Susan, who had, with her now-estranged and departed husband, developed and tended and invested her spirit in this land. We sent her energy to be strong, to be centered, to do what and as she needed to. We sang songs to the land herself, loving her independently of owning her. Greenbo spoke of a need for a connection to be made directly between us and Susan. At one point LaRosa said she saw a crab swimming in the bowl of water in front of her, signifying to her the sun in Cancer. Then I, knowing nothing of astrological signs and months except for my own birthday, divined that on July 7th something important was going to happen about this land. My circle-sisters were intrigued, and somewhat amused, as I insisted that on that exact date, no matter what else was happening in my life, I was going to be in contact with Risa, if only to say hello!

Because we had sent so much energy to Susan and the land, it seemed too strange to us to never have met her, so Bethroot and I decided to write to Susan. We suggested that we visit her the next time we were out doing realtor work. She responded, wrote it was OK for us to stop by if we were in the area, though it would not suit her for well over a month.

Bethroot continued her correspondence with realtors and we both continued our meditations. I went to stay with friends at the Fishpond for a month, and went to my first peyote circle. In a tipi in the back canyon at Cabbage Lane, twelve of us women-loving-women, filled with the power of mescalita, touched by something ancient, womanly, magical, sang songs of strength and love throughout the long night. How that circle did center me, and free my spirit!

Mid-June Bethroot went out on a land search: she talked with all the realtors in yet another small town, and went to see a few parcels, none of which was right for us. A card from Susan said we could stop in on Sunday June 27th, so I went to meet Bethroot that morning. As we started walking up the long hill, we asked ourselves why we were doing this, taking another look at what we wanted and could not have? To remind ourselves, we agreed, of our goal of such beauty, which must exist elsewhere as well. We reached the hilltop ready to have a friendly visit with Susan, who spoke of having arrived at a clear determination to stick it out, to go ahead with her plans for this land. In this context, we shared with her our love for her home. We walked in the garden and talked of her successes there, we marveled at her stories about the construction of the round house, we learned from her about water systems and early homesteaders. "You'll find your land," Susan encouraged. "Oh yes," we smiled back, "it can't be far off now." And she promised if ever she did change her mind and decide to sell, we'd be the first to know.

I felt so light and happy as we started back down the hill: we had completed something in finally visiting with Susan, giving the whole experience a circularity where it had felt so linear. It is also true that I was still deeply bonded with the land, with the dancing woman, my vision of my life there still strong and clear. I knew I was in the middle of a contradiction, but I did not dwell on that. I just felt good about Susan, and about my vision.

The next day Bethroot and I looked at an eighty-acre parcel with a good price, friendly neighbors, plenty of water, but no development at all. We hiked around on that land most of the day trying to make it be where we could settle, despite the drawbacks – we were becoming desperate to stop looking for land and start living on it. But this land did not answer our songs, or at least we could not hear them, and we knew it was not the right place. We parted again, Bethroot to go back to the realtor circuit, and I to the tipi at Cabbage Lane, where I had just begun what was supposed to be a month's stay.

A couple of evenings later, Bethroot saw another rainbow on the horizon, at Rainbow's End where she was visiting. It was, again, a catalyst for hope, and sure enough the next morning she got a phone call from Risa relaying Susan's decision to sell to us after all! She had liked us a lot, was moved by our love for this land, and after thinking it over for a couple days, felt she could part with it now. She was excited to be doing this, needed to let go of the past, to make a fresh start in her life. When Bethroot brought this news to me I was stunned in spite of my foreknowing; it took the whole day to get over my resistance to trusting that Susan would not change her mind again. I did not want any more disappointments.

The following Sunday we climbed the hill to visit Susan again, and yes, it was true! We had another happy afternoon together. Then Wednesday was the first day we were able to go to Risa's office to draw up the formal offer: the date was July 7th.

The next few weeks were full of worry and hassle working out the unromantic but necessary details of the sale: what was to be included, what wasn't, clearing up easement questions, determining the pace of the changeover. The business of transitioning from land-search and making an offer, to actual land-purchase brought into sharp relief Bethroot's and my fears and differences, as well as some ambivalence about living together we hadn't given much attention to. It was one thing to carry a vision together, quite another to sign on the line to a twenty-year mortgage and anticipate moving to land without electricity, or telephone, over an hour's drive from the nearest dykes we knew. We each had to take mighty deep breaths, interspersed with anxious gasps, as we labored and processed our way toward a contract with Susan and with each other we thought we could live with.

Energy poured in from friends everywhere in those days, helping us to stay clear and trust we were on the road. One woman in California did special meditations for us to ease the hassle, another wrote of possible sources of loans, still others sent words of strength and caring. The land sale contract was finally signed, and we breathed more easily, though we could not move onto the land until August 20th.

In the following weeks I visited friends to the north and south, and stretched my welcome at Cabbage Lane, while Bethroot finished her commitment at the motel and then went up to Portland. I weathered one crisis after another: the clutch went out on my pickup, I had to care for an alcoholic woman's nineteen dogs who were camped out on a nearby hill while she went to a detox center, I got badly stung by wasps, it rained for days and the tipi leaked. I was on overload, just hanging on until I could get to that hilltop and collapse. Meanwhile, Bethroot attended a weekend-long Lifespring seminar, an offshoot of EST, both part of the popular Growth Movement. The emotional intensity of those days

strained her own overload to the breaking point and she ended up
in a crisis clinic soon after the seminar. So, instead of getting off
the Interstate at Myrtle Creek on August 20th, I headed for
Portland, where I joined with a large circle of women who had
rallied to monitor and assist Bethroot through this episode. It was
not until the 30th that Lavy, Phyrste, and I finally arrived at the
land, when Bethroot was past the crisis but still healing in the
hospital.

Things were awfully uncertain as I entered what I had been
holding as paradise. Seeing all there was to tend, to manage, to
clean, was overwhelming. I was grateful when evening came,
grateful for the dusky blanket that obscured the daylight's demands
and let me relax into the present, trust in a secure future. I sat on
the edge of the trailer porch into the night as the moon headed to
the west and washed me with the promise of beauty and magic.
As I sat there I felt a presence behind me on the porch, not
something frightening, but commanding. I slowly turned and welcomed the slow and steady approach of a small calico cat, who
stepped into the moonshine on my lap as though she had always
done so. She rubbed against me and spoke a gentle meow, which
I understood as a welcome, as an announcement that I had passed
a test she must have been conducting from the shadows as night
fell. Our bonding was instantaneous. I called her Moonshine.

I pushed myself to make several more supportive, and exhausting, trips back and forth to Portland while Bethroot steadily
improved. By mid-September she made her belated but happy
arrival, and added Missy to the calico's name.

The sunny Autumn of 1976 gave us psychic rest and renewal,
and we took on the challenges of the land, working most days
until we dropped, often with help from visiting friends. We had the
road graded, ditched, rocked, and graded again, then fine-tuned it
with picks and hoes and shovels; canned and stored what was left
in the garden and the apple orchard; covered the plywood exterior
of the house with heavy black felt; used Big Blue, the 3/4 ton
Dodge which came with the land, to haul truckloads of manure

from a neighbor's barnyard to enrich our garden; and much more. We often became overrun by how much we had to do, how much we had to learn in order to do it. We realized we underestimated the cost of nearly everything. The road repair, tools, chicken feed, unexpected repairs on autos, the trailer and water system, and a gargantuan list of "miscellaneous" played havoc with our budget. Our hopes for a witches' gathering in the big house on Hallowmas gave way to the realization that it would be some time before we could earn and save enough money to make that structure usable, as well as restore the barn, or replace the sagging garden fence, and on and on the list went. Sometimes we became frustrated and dull-hearted with the work and money worries, dissatisfied with each other's preferences and habits, and lost sight of our spiritual purpose. But always something or someone came along to clear our vision. Musawa Seaweed gave us a small prism which Bethroot hung on the garden gate – a special reminder of the sacredness of growth, ours as well as the plants'. Entering the garden became an invitation to put aside our quarrels about what to plant where or what was best for mulch, and to remember: this place, your life, are holy. We started the practice of beginning each evening's meal with holding hands and singing, a ritual to remind us that song was available to us all day on this hilltop where echoes join in. We had our first circle with our Rainbow's End sisters, a deepening of the connection between us and the lands we love.

We asked the land her name, tried on "Sun Dancing Land," then "High Farm," finally understood she is *Fly Away Home*, from a favorite circle song: "One bright morning as we work together/ love each other/ sing together, gonna fly away home. . . ."

*   *   *

At a mid-October sunrise I stand on a large log. The sky shines pink and gold through countless puffs of clouds on my left, the moon – just past full – nears the horizon on my right. All in motion, constantly changing, making beauty out of beauty. I stand and sing, and weep with happiness. I am here, I am home at last.

And the Last Shall Be Phyrste

So tired . . . and it is only just noon. This old stuffed chair never felt more comfortable, nor its cushioned stool more welcoming of my exhausted legs. Phyrste snores, resting peacefully on his pillow near the warm woodstove. Missy Moonshine is not to be seen just now, but one of her daughters, Sami Slate, purrs on my lap, while the other, Lillith One, lies stretched out on the living-room rug near Phyrste. Ladydog sleeps on the floor beside my chair; her sidekick, Mailava, chases dream rabbits on her bed. A few yards from the window, primroses bloom gaily on Lavy's month-old grave.

Phyrste had another seizure around midnight last night – it started in his sleep, several hours after we had gone to bed. He would not rest afterwards, so I carried him downstairs where he could walk the circle of the house for a while, not having to worry about awakening anyone, because Bethroot and Bonnie are up in Portland for the weekend. Izetta, my mate of these last five years, is up there too, making a new life for herself. Without me. While Phyrste paced, I curled up in the big green chair, listened to the night tell me of my loneliness, and drifted into memories.

So many changes these almost eight years since Bethroot and I began our commitment with this land. We realized early on that we each had many needs the other could not meet, sometimes roughly pulling in opposite directions to satisfy them, sometimes pulling together to bring more love and laughter to our lives. And joy did come, in many guises. Missy Moonshine surprised us with a litter of entertaining kittens that first Spring, then nearly a year later the collie, Ladydog, joined our animal family. A woman who had taken "Women in Transition," a community education class I taught in town back then, asked me to temporarily care for the elegant big dog until she got resettled with her two teenage daughters in a bigger city upstate. There had been a mutual attraction between us, but Lesbianism was more transition than she could handle. I knew Lady was here to stay, and counted myself the richer: "Lassie" had come home, a solace for the loss of the storybook magnificence Caius had been.

Love and laughter . . . and music, magic, drama, passion. All this came as both Bethroot and I determinedly opened ourselves to other women.

I first saw Izetta, originally a theater-friend of Bethroot's from Portland, singing lead soprano in the *Izquierda Ensemble*. The group, founded by old friends of ours, did a concert in Eugene, over two hours' drive north of here. The richness and fullness of her voice, the way the notes seemed to pulse through her whole small body, the subtle shyness I sensed in her sharp features and quiet eyes, kept me riveted all through the concert. Izetta came for a visit during our third Autumn, delighted us with her gift for costumery and ritual at our first grand Hallowmas gathering, in the yet unfinished, but heated, house. By Winter I had found my emotional and sexual yearnings matched by hers. I was dazzled by her intensity, her depth, the power of her will, the beauty of her song. I was flip-flop-belly in love, pulled out all my psychic and emotional stops, and projected a mating to last into old age.

Izetta loved this land and the beauty of what we had begun here. She brought her musical skill and imagination to our ritual singing circles, let herself lean into my devotion, my home-making. With my earth-solid practicality and her fiery inventiveness, my dependable drone to her inspiring riff, my jet-black hair and her blond, we made a striking pair. We both wanted this loving, wanted it fiercely enough to carry the burden of its contradictions: she had a young son; I was deeply committed to honoring this land, and my being, as woman-only space. The boy was living with his father, but Izetta saw him often and had him with her for school vacations. She ached to live here, was herself drawn to this Separatist vision of women making our own culture, with ritual, muscle and sweat, and thought she could juggle all the callings of her life. Her son, her professional singing and touring, as well as theater productions, old friends and lovers in Portland, all pulled on her as strongly as this land. She would home here, and leave for weeks, sometimes months, at a time. Often that meant I would leave for short times to be with her, stretching myself back to the city, taking on again the pace I had desperately left behind over three years before.

Sometimes Izetta and I blended the work of the land and the work of the wider world into a productive, if not always easy, harmony. And sometimes the dissonance of our commitments and longings felt like lightning cracking between us. We each craved for the other to be the person we were lonely for: I, a stay-at-home land-tending lover, mate; Izetta, a co-parent who genuinely loved her son. My disappointment was thick and no doubt suffocating, Izetta's explosive anger often a swinging sword. And through it all we kept coming back to each other, to our passion, to this home, to a fantasy of it all working out somehow, some year.

The focused intensity between Izetta and me was sometimes too much for Bethroot to bear, so she moved temporarily back to Portland to work with a theater company. When Izetta was doing her city scene as well, I was home alone. Though at times overwhelmed with all the responsibility of managing this home, I did welcome the peaceful simple solitude with the dogs, cats, chickens, trees, sky, silence.

During one of those spells when I was here alone mid-Autumn, Bonnie, a young woman travelling through, came to visit for several days. She took to this land right off, and I enjoyed her small compact energy, her gentle presence, her warmth with the animals, her appreciation of the garden. Within a few months she wrote from back East with a request to come live here by late the following Spring. I was delighted with the prospect of being accompanied by her exuberance for this physically demanding life, and her careful ways. For her part, Bethroot was glad she would have company when she completed her stay in the city and I left to be with Izetta, and, reluctantly, her son, for several weeks.

So then we were four, in various combinations, at various times. One of the first projects the four of us did, when we were all here together, was to erect the teepee Bonnie had borrowed from a friend. She cleared brush from the site she had chosen up the hill, then we all maneuvered the long heavy poles into place, and draped the huge awkward canvas over them. In the next days Bonnie made a sturdy platform for her bed, shelves, an altar, a rock-lined firepit, creating simple beauty in a safe and efficient space. Any qualms I may have had about sharing this land with a near-total stranger were put to rest by her prudence and ingenuity.

Izetta mostly shared my high inner circle bedroom with me, but soon needed a space of her own, so she and I walled off half of the gatehouse, installed a couple of windows and a door with a glass panel, and turned it into a private getaway for her, heated by the Jötul woodstove she had brought with her, a leftover from a country season she had had in her straight life. When she had moved in her belongings, including the steamer trunk which had been her grandmother's, an actress of some fame in the twenties, and decorated the room to her liking, she invited us all to come dressed in costumes for an evening of room-warming, playing characters that expressed something relevant to the occasion of her taking on this life. Bonnie came as a Packi Rodén, a French-speaking packrat, extending the welcome of the forest creatures. Bethroot played Rebecca Keaton, a composite of her Tennessee country forbears, a strong woman who knows how to do hard work and make family. I dressed as a nun, of a Lesbian feminist variety, welcoming and honoring what stirred in Izetta to want to share this Separatist life. Izetta hosted us as Jewel, a twangy, somewhat pugilistic version of the part of Izetta who chafed at woman-only space. It was a raucous evening, as we all got a little tipsy on the brandy Izetta served. The alcohol gave us permission to voice our doubts about what the four of us could make here together, as well as celebrate the possibilities.

Within the year Bethroot and Bonnie became lovers, and the dynamics shifted and complexified. Then Bonnie came home from the county fair with a fluffy auburn puppy, so Mailava joined our menagerie as we all grew ourselves into a family. During the school year, when Izetta could be here for long stretches, we four had fun working to finish and sparsely furnish the interior of the house, erect a new garden fence, cut and haul firewood, prune the orchard. And we wrangled too, mostly over the *how* of things, not so much the *why*. Four strong-minded women were bound to butt our heads now and again, requiring long exhausting sessions of processing, hours of deliberations and emotings, before many decisions could be made. We wove song throughout it all, crafting a four-part harmony that began each supper and sometimes filled the dark Winter evenings.

We shared the magic of marijuana and mushrooms, and led each other through Days of Intention, with special forest walks, special food. We opened our rituals at the Solstices and Equinoxes to the dozens of women who came to fill the center of the round house. We held weekend workshops in Personal Theater and Tai Chi. Last year we doggedly rehearsed, then performed, for audiences of women up and down the Oregon slice of the Interstate, a play we three had urged Bethroot to write. *Feathers in My Mind* was part her personal history, including her mother's illness and death in 1972, and part a celebration of our country Lesbian family-making.

It was a life full to overflowing with all that Bethroot and I had envisioned, plus much we had not. The struggles among the four of us sometimes cost more than the love and friendship reimbursed. My increased travelling back and forth to the city, the stress and noise, drummed at my already failing hearing, exacerbated the ringing in my ears, and kept me in an agonizing limbo. Izetta was sometimes stretched in agony between the unreconciled poles of her life. The tension between us often erupted into ugly scenes which took too much time and attention to heal. Bonnie began the process of moving beyond the limits of this isolation, needing to explore her talents as an artist, with teachers and facilities only a city school could provide. Bethroot, always the Libra, did well to balance herself through all our pushings and pullings, though she fought with her demons of jealousy and incipient loneliness.

It has occurred more than once in my life that when things become stressed to the point of breaking, something happens that changes the very nature of the struggle, something unforeseeable, a *dea ex machina* who picks up the elements of the scene and rearranges them, requiring the players to make life-changing adjustments. Which is what happened on Valentine's Day of '83. We all had just returned the night before from performing Bethroot's play in Eugene, the last on a three-city tour. We had done our work beautifully, moved many scores of women with our theater, as well as our comradery as a troupe. But the stresses of travelling and performing took their toll, and we were all tired and irritable by the time we returned home. I was so glad to be sleeping in my own bed again, Izetta snuggled beside me. In the dim half-sleep of morning, I heard Izetta get up, then quietly ask, "Will you be my Valentine?" "Umm . . . hmmm," I answered through smiling lips.

Later that morning she and I were stretching in the downstairs inner circle, working out the kinks left from the tour, returning our bodies to the routines of this country life. Izetta heard the crunch of a car's tires out on the lane, and through a window we soon saw Judith, a dyke friend from Myrtle Creek whose phone number we gave out for emergency messages, rushing toward the house. The news she bore thundered into our lives. Our Valentine turned into a volcano: Izetta's son's father had died from a heart attack that morning. The friend caring for the boy was awaiting a call from Izetta.

She and I rushed off to use the nearest neighbor's phone,

arrangements were made, and as we drove back up the hill, with plans to leave immediately on the seven-hour drive to her son, I knew Izetta would leave me. I could feel her insides turning away from *Fly Away Home*, away from this life which could no longer work for her, away from our bond. I said nothing of this, concentrated on the task at hand, and kept the throbbing in my chest from breaking into my throat.

Curled in the darkness in the chair, I was remembering that throbbing keenly when Phyrste, finally worn out from his pacing, came to my lap. His warm small body was a comfort in the night, his needs a welcome present focus away from the painful memory. We both dozed for a while, then I carried him back up to bed, where sleep eased us to a pale Winter's dawn.

We awoke fairly early, were up by 6:30. Phyrste seemed his normal strong self so I gently pushed him out the doggie door, then returned to my room to dress. I have been doing this the last few mornings: seeing that he has good command of his legs, and tending to indoor things for a few minutes while he poops and comes back into the house under his own steam.

Perhaps I took a little longer than usual this morning. I was sad and weary after the late night's rememberings, moved slowly into my sweats and flannels, had a little trouble getting the larger logs to catch in the woodstove. When I went outside to look for him, Phyrste was gone. I told myself not to panic – this has happened before and he has always reappeared, quietly hobbling back from the pooper path, or sneakily ensconced on his pillow. And each time I have lived through mental horrors of what could have happened to him. Phyrste – epileptic, lame in his hind legs, easily confused, poor eyesight and hearing, over a hundred years old. But this morning I determined to remain calm, even tended the stove on one of my double-checks into the house, picked some kale down in the barnyard's Winter garden, checked out the temporary protection we had laid on the pooper roof. But no Phyrste anywhere.

It was on the way to the gatehouse, where some of Izetta's clothes and her grandmother's trunk yet remain, when the fear started to swell in me, and on the way back when I began to wail. And all the while, Lady and Mailava acted like two puppies on a pleasure stroll, heedless to my pleas for them to find Phyrste. At the sound of my crying they seemed embarrassed, as though scolded for their play. Back to the house again – no Phyrste lying on his pillow looking at me in surprise as if to say "What's all the fuss?" More attention to the stove and then I'm off again, panting and sweating from the now-frantic search. I would either get in my pickup and drive down our mile-and-a-quarter road, or else hike past the pooper to the east side of our forty acres. He wandered in those two directions sometimes; did he simply forget to turn around? My decision as to which way to go was made by an intense need to erase my growing feeling of helplessness, catapulting me in any direction so long as I was *doing* something, rather than just staring at the ground in shock. Now was when I surely needed there to be the four of us again: Bonnie with her keen hearing and quick energy, Izetta's perseverance, Bethroot's compassion. But I was alone with this crisis: Phyrste was out there somewhere and I had to find him.

I told Mailava and Lady to stay around the house so the noise of their rough-housing would not cover up anything I might be able to hear, and set off on foot toward the east side. With sudden poignancy I knew the truth of translating "disabled" into "physically challenged": the tinnitus and hearing loss made me give up trying to hear all but the loudest bird calls a long time ago, and here I was straining to pick up any sound which would guide me to Phyrste. I was about halfway to the pooper when indeed I did hear a strange sound in the forest, faint and downhill from me. But I could not tell for sure what direction it was coming from, something I have a lot of difficulty with under normal conditions. This sound was clearly an animal in distress. I called Phyrste and whistled. The sound got louder. I knew this sound – it was Phyrste's: a cross between a groan and a whimper, the only sound he makes anymore, save for his quite audible snoring. The anguished call from the forest was Phyrste's voice magnified to a whimpering groaning scream. Another rush of adrenalin coursed through me and I went running down past the pooper and into the forest a short way, calling and listening. He seemed a little further away but I got clearer on the direction. I figured I should not go down into the forest there, but return to the house and descend from that point.

But what if I made the wrong decision? Could I trust my ears? I felt the grief in me that comes from not being perfect when someone I love needs me to do it right. I had tried for so many months to be a loyal and supportive companion for Izetta, as she, frightened and unprepared, took on full-time the world of her ten-year-old son. But no matter how hard I worked at it, how much I stretched beyond my own fears and limitations, how negligent I eventually became of my own needs in favor of hers, I failed to be the partner Izetta wanted and deserved. We were tied to each other with a desperate need that muted wisdom, while at the same time she persisted in creating a home, inventing a life, with no place for the real me in it. I finally had to accept that she belonged with, and to, not me, but her son. And I did not.

Now Phyrste needed me, and I was determined to be effective as precisely who I am. I raced back to the house where Lady and Mailava waited. They shyly joined me and followed me to the woods behind the house. I whistled again – the answer was louder now. The other two finally registered what I had been hearing; a team at last, the three of us began the descent into the forest. I was shocked at how steep the drop was there, sickened at the thought of Phyrste tumbling down, out of control. It was a long way down to that sound. Down, down we went, following the call, the pace as fast as I could go, running from tree to tree, stopping periodically to check the direction, the cry ever louder. At the very bottom of the ravine – we had gone south and east – a seasonal creek rolled loudly down its narrow course. There, in a hollow made by rotted logs, in a small pool of icy rushing water, just below a knee-high waterfall, stood my dear Phyrste, soaked, shivering and howling as effectively as he could. I collapsed on the bank and cried as I pulled him out of what would have been a permanent trap for his aging body.

I cradled him against my wool mackinaw for a few minutes, wanting my body to warm his, needing to gain my breath, steady my legs. I knew I was deeper in that ravine than I had ever gone; it was a long way back up, an arduous enough task alone, and I was going to have to carry Phyrste's thirty pounds. Maybe it would be easier to step over the creek and ascend on the east slope. I already knew the west slope would be hard, the east couldn't be any harder.

Phyrste's intense shivering and now soft moaning pushed me up and walking, climbing. It took me a long time, with frequent stops to sit and pant, and sense which way to trudge through the trees and brush. I kept thinking I had seen the east side path, only to find more forest. Lady and Mailava stayed close to me, following my lead through the unfamiliar terrain. At last we did emerge, at the far south edge of the east side. My arms and shoulders ached from carrying Phyrste, but when I put him down he bent over in a quivering wet mass, unable to move, so I lifted him to my chest again and started off on the relatively easy, well-known path. I felt like the shepherd with the little lost lamb in the stained glass church window of my childhood's Sunday mornings. Back then I had identified with the lamb, and last night's memories had conjured a similar feeling. But now I was the shepherd, and, following the example in that window, hoisted Phyrste across my shoulders. I would be strong enough to bear this burden, and more.

It took about an hour of towelling Phyrste and bundling him inside an afghan and a down jacket before his shivering subsided. I lay exhausted beside him on the floor a few minutes and nuzzled his face with mine. He licked my nose in what I understood as a sweet thank you. "I love you, Phyrste," I cooed back, then came to the comfort of the old chair.

Some years ago a woman told me the story of how she had found her dogfriend in the forest trapped in a hole that had caved in on her. I marvelled at that story, at the success where failure was so easy, at the bond between woman and dog acting like a magnet between them. I taste that marvel again and look gratefully at Phyrste snoring on his pillow, dry, full-bellied, content. Something is going right in my life, something full of truth, goodness, and beauty, something full of peace and love.

Champ and the Butterfly

The early June morning was bright and crisp as I drove down the hill with outgoing mail and my breakfast. I turned my pickup around and left it just inside our closed gate, then crossed the county road to put my letters into the big black metal mailbox, and turn up the red flag to signal a stop for the postwoman. Back across the road again, I settled close to a small clump of flowering red clover near the gate to eat my predictable soaked oats, chopped apples, seeds, and yoghurt. I had brought my camera along and thought to make some pictures while I waited for the rural-route delivery to get this far out from town. When I had first arrived, a large black and white butterfly hovered about the clover, so I had my camera ready and sat peacefully breakfasting.

I had been at serious photography for about only a year, since friends pooled to buy me a camera for my forty-fifth birthday in 1984. My growing collection of portraits of still-life flowers, trees, the old barn, the ridges, and other such unresisting objects, was pleasing. I could count on their availability whenever I felt like taking a break from the daily routine of landwork and play with lenses, light and shadow. I certainly was not bored with these subjects, but I had been wondering about learning more patience, about waiting for the unanticipated to come to me, for wild creatures to come close enough to my trustworthy eye.

Patience had not been one of my recent virtues. After tending Phyrste for many months until he finally died in my arms from old age, I was at my wit's end as to how to help poor ailing Missy Moonshine. I had studied my home remedy books, offered her special foods and supplements, had her checked out and medicated by the vet in town, but she nonetheless continued to weaken, her sweet little calico body getting thinner every week. And another request had come from Izetta for a few of the things she had not yet taken; with each departing item I felt abandoned all over again. I grew impatient for her to take all of her things and be done with it, rather than go through the break-up each time an afghan, or a chair, or a favorite pewter plate left my singleness for hers. I certainly was ready for something wild and unanticipated to at least interrupt the pattern of defeat in which I felt stuck.

The butterfly teased me from an out-of-camera-range distance, disappeared entirely for a while. I was sitting only a few yards from South Myrtle Creek Road, where logging trucks roared down the mountain with their loads of cedar and fir, the empty trucks shifting gears on their piggy-back return to the forest. The assaulting noise, every ten minutes or so, in both directions, was not very conducive to learning patience.

Across the road the hill rose high, bearing the countenance of re-greening after the neighbor's logging a few years back. The Scotch Broom had given a yellow laughter to the hill and the grasses softened the face of the narrow valley shouldering the tree-lined creek.

Suddenly I heard a hound baying on the hill. It takes some will power to not be overly alarmed at that sound – a dog can seem very distressed when howling at its quarry, which I assumed was the scenario beyond my sight. I held to my place on the hard ground, slowly chewed sunflower seeds, and continued to wait for the butterfly . . . but not for long, as the dog's calling became more plaintive than aggressive, and my attempt at detachment faltered. I was pulled to investigate, so crossed the road and walked at a gentle pace, half on a rescue mission, half on a photographer's search for pictures, the little wildflowers beckoning brightly after the rain of the week before. I listened, and looked, and continued to eat from my bowl.

Hearing the dog again, I whistled Caius's whistle – I didn't think he'd mind, already dead nine years; besides, it had become

Ladydog's whistle too, with a rather all-purpose melody to it. I whistled again, then I heard the people: first an angry voice of a man, demanding with volume: "Champ! C'mere, boy, c'mon!" Sometimes he would disguise his irate frustration with a solicitous "good buddy." Apparently this didn't work, as a second, then a third voice took the place of his: a young woman's voice, then another woman's, each calling cheerfully, imploringly, for Champ. I felt a little embarrassed, exposed, intruded upon, just a step removed from how I'd feel if I heard strangers shouting that close if I were standing up on our secluded knoll, or beside the house, tucked within the safety of our women's sanctuary, instead of down here near the public road, strolling in the neighbor's forest.

With my zoom lens I focused on the movement I noticed about halfway up the hill. Sure enough: a liver-spotted hound dog was making his way down the steep hillside, threading through thicket and fallen trees. I could not tell if the voices were coming from the ridge top or down near the creek, but the dog looked happy in his descent, as though headed towards someone whose call was pleasing. When he entered the stand of small trees bordering the creek, I could no longer see him, so I walked on toward the creek bed, further downstream than I had explored before.

A movement high on the ridge caught my attention: what I had thought were three small trees transformed into three people turning away from their overlook. "They've lost their dog," I thought. Maybe they had been searching for days for this lost pet, maybe it was the same hound I had heard baying in the forest over towards White Rock Road a few days before. Poor fella: the valley walls must have echoed the calls and he, confused, went in the wrong direction in pursuit of his people. My whistling now became a strong friendly invitation to be found.

I was surprised to discover the creek banks were extremely steep, twenty feet of near-vertical slant, with deer trails making diagonals through the thick brush. I called the hound and was answered by the clanking of a bell, similar to a small cow's bell. Then I saw the dog, walking and lapping up water in the creek bed. "Hey, Champ! Hiya!" I reached like an old friend, amused to find ourselves here. I didn't think he would be able to get up to me on that steep bank and wondered if we could meet further upstream, where I knew the bank was more accessible. I underestimated him, however, for he made little of the climb and soon was hungrily eating the last of my morning meal, while I spoke a welcome and rubbed my palm on his smooth freckled head.

Those three on the ridge must have known the area well, for soon I saw a pickup slowing down out on South Myrtle, probably aiming for the turn-out at the green wooden gate which sentinels the bottom of our road. I jangled the bell on Champ's collar to let them know where we were, to speed the glad reunion. He clearly did not like the sound of that bell, gently moved his chin over my hand to make me stop. I could not blame him – how awful to have that clanging in his ears, similar, I supposed, to the tinnitus that rings constantly in mine. I savored that moment we had alone then, a simple spontaneous comradery kindled by hunger and concern.

I was glad when it was the mother and her teen-age daughter who appeared first. I recognized the older woman from behind the counter in the Western Auto in town fifteen miles away. This was their dog all right, though there was more scolding in their voices than greeting. The man came with a leash and pulled the dog to a willow bush. The talking among us was fast and friendly, strangers taking care of business.

"I hate it when he has to whip 'em," the woman spoke somewhat apologetically, and the daughter explained, a-little-too-quickly, how it was "necessary," in order to train the hounds not to take off after deer and then refuse to come back. I wondered what lessons she had been taught with similar methods. Apparently Champ had heard the direction of their calling after all, and had chosen its opposite, heading toward me and my waiting breakfast bowl, and soft hands. The willow wand smacked against the dog's side, his yelps echoing the distress I had interpreted from the baying earlier. I did not have much to say after that, except to point out that this "training method" obviously did not work if indeed the dog had been beaten before and had just then disobeyed. So much for rescue missions and glad reunions.

I walked back up to their pickup with them and met the three other hounds in the large wooden crate that was their home-on-the-road. Without waiting for permission, I reached through the small windows and touched them all in mutual greeting, including the one who had apparently forgotten he was, according to the man, "too shy" around strangers. I silently blessed the dogs and, although I love the deer and am in awe of the black bears the hounds are trained to pursue, I honored their desire to run, the basic instinct in them to chase and nourish themselves. The wild life in them feeding upon wildlife.

After they had all gone I sat in my pickup for a few minutes, gathering myself back in, re-settling myself, my camera still hanging from my neck. I thought of the restraints and limitations in my life, the times I had wanted to run free from responsibilities, escape the fetters of disappointment and pain. I was about to give up waiting for the day's mail and return home, when the black and white butterfly swooped over the gate and approached the red clover. I quietly got out of my truck, slowly followed her, and made three easy portraits as she posed spread-wing on a flower.

"Thank you," I whispered, "for your patience," and drove back up the hill.

Visit/Visitation

I first noticed her when I went outside to do my early morning chore of opening the little door of the henhouse, to free the chickens for their day of ranging. The little brown bird sat motionless on the walkway to the deck I built last Spring, her eyes closed, her feathers fluffed out against the morning cold, looking like meditative pregnancy. So strange: a wild bird in such quiet repose, just sitting there a few feet from me. I talked very gently to her, fearing she might be startled and fly away. But her stillness continued, even as I crept in slow motion to where she sat, drawing myself close to her. I was amazed at her apparent trust, as with one finger I delicately stroked her downy cream-mottled chest. She opened her eyes slowly, her bottom eyelids moving down to reveal the small dark orbs. She looked at me as though to acknowledge my presence, then pulled the lids up again, assuming an air of undisturbed serenity. I'd never heard of such behavior, and I worried that she was sick – although she looked a healthy plump – or maybe injured. I didn't want to leave her there in the chill, an easy prey for Sami Slate. We repeated the stroking-eyeing communication and I ever so carefully picked her up with both hands and held her against my warm cotton-clothed chest. Suspending disbelief, and containing my great delight, I carried her up to my room to my desk. Sami Slate lay on the bed nearby, purring when I talked to her. I explained this little bird was a friend I was tending, and Sami showed no interest in interfering. The wren looked up at me, then lay against my chest in contentment as I wrote in my journal.

Wednesday, September 18

My mother's plane was a half-hour late. I waited in the small airport restaurant with a glass of milk and a plate of french fries, not quite believing myself: haven't had french fries in many years. It crossed my mind to steal away from my seat at the counter before the waitress reappeared from the kitchen with the greasy fried potatoes, but I was too embarrassed, compelled by a sense of morality learned early in my Lutheran childhood. Later I decided the carbohydrates and milk and pure pleasure were just what I needed before seeing my mother again. It had been two years since we last saw each other (and fifteen before then). Two years ago there were four of us to welcome Rita, when my sister shepherded her on a flight from the East Coast to southern Oregon, for that busy ten-day reunion, a few years after my father died. Now just Bethroot and I live here, my lover and hers both moved back to the city. There will be lots of space to fill up in the coming two weeks.

Through the wall of windows in the waiting room, I watched Rita descend the mobile staircase from the plane and walk across the concrete to the terminal. She sported a beige polyester pants-suit, carried her knitting bag, and walked with a sense that the earth is her natural habitat. Her white hair looked freshly curled. *This woman is attractive*, I thought, and made a point of telling her so, a number of times, as we hugged excitedly and then during the long drive north to my secluded hilltop home. She protested, of course, considering her one hundred and eighty pounds on her seventy-year-old 5'3" frame very unappealing. But I think my mother liked her daughter telling her otherwise.

The two-hour drive was full of easy talking, though we were both quite tired by the time we reached Myrtle Creek and the grocery shopping we had yet to do. Fifteen more miles out from town, and up our road through the neighbor's timber forest, and we were gladly home. I was deeply thankful for the relative silence, and Rita was glad for the earth to stop moving as it had been since early morning, when she began her journey from Pennsylvania. We joined Bethroot for a dinner of our home-grown vegetables, and the rhubarb-blackberry-apple pie I baked yesterday for dessert. And Rita presented me with my Christmas gift already: a beautiful patchwork quilt she worked on all last Winter.

Thursday, September 19

Rita chafes a bit at having to be silent and basically on her own all morning, though she is understanding and compassionate about my need for some hours of quiet solitude in order to handle our catching-up chatting all afternoon and evening. Many things have changed in my life since that visit two years ago: in addition to my mate's leaving, Lavy and Phyrste and Missy Moonshine have all died; Bethroot and I are not always so easy with each other as we used to be; some of my spiritual vision and love of life have been eroded. Rita noticed I have a few more grey hairs among the black I inherited from her, and that my hearing has worsened a little in the past two years. By the end of today my hyperacusive ears were sore from so much unaccustomed talking and listening, and I was glad for silence again after Rita went to bed in the trailer.

I am suddenly aware the word *Lesbian* comes up quite often in normal conversation here. I wonder what Rita's internal response is when that happens. Her face reveals nothing, and she is mute on the subject thus far. Similarly, when she mentions her much adored son, my brother who beat me regularly without her interference or even effective disapproval, I do not respond overtly. I let it pass, like the energy I deflect as I do Tai Chi each morning.

Friday, September 20

I asked Rita to talk to me about her mother, my "mamaw," Mary Gertrude, who died when I was about a year old, leaving me no memory of her at all. I've heard this story before, one Rita and my aunts and uncles would sometimes go over together when the family gathered for a holiday supper. I know she likes to talk about her mother, and I welcome even this fragile sense of my matrilineage.

Mamaw had an extremely hard life, physically and emotionally. One of thirteen children, she had to take over mothering responsibilities when yet a teenager. Eventually the family fell apart, the children put in foster homes here and there. . . . The story becomes heart-wrenching as Rita describes the siblings searching for each other until they are all under one roof again.

Rita spoke of her mother as a "saint" who only once ever lifted a hand to her, when Rita had said something smart-alecky and Mamaw "smacked" her across the face. The novelty of the scene struck them both funny, Rita said, such that they both burst out laughing. I wonder what my mother computes when she thinks of her saintly mother who never hit her, and remembers when she herself hit me often, and viciously. I suppose the implication is that I deserved it, I was so bad. But I know better.

Saturday, September 21, Autumn Equinox

At noon, at the end of morning silence, we had lunch on the deck, where Rita loves to sit and enjoy my many flower boxes and the expansive view of distant ridges. As we ate I noticed a fine, thin, gold chain bracelet she was wearing and asked her about it. She related it had belonged to a dear friend of hers who had given it to her before she died a year and a half ago, and she has worn it on her wrist ever since. I told her I would like to have the bracelet after she died, so I could picture something she has that I want, something which would be close to her in the years to come, which would soak up the spirit of her and come to me after her death. She was pleased with my request and readily agreed to it.

It was a beautiful sunny day. In the afternoon about twenty women came to our Equinox celebration, as well as to honor Bethroot's birthday and give blessings to the yurt, her private space up the hill. Then there was a potluck in the house. It was a delight to see a dozen or so women all in the kitchen I've built, doing various tasks, no one uncomfortable or crowded. Lots more came by the time we had an evening of singing so we were a large group, a very rousing and willing group. I had a good time, appreciated the presence of so many Lesbians to give my mother more of the context and content of my life. Rita joined in on a familiar song now and again, seemed to enjoy herself. But I wasn't certain about how she felt, and what she thought, in the company of so many Lesbians, a couple of whom were close to her in age. I did not look at her very much, wanted to be feasting on the presence of the women of my community. I did notice several times women sat on the floor beside the high-backed rocker where Rita spent the evening, and made conversation with her. But I could not tell what she was feeling. Late in the evening, as we all sang "la-la" to a melody not many of us knew the words for, she looked relaxed, lay her head back on the rocker and closed her eyes. I made my singing into a lullaby for her.

Sunday, September 22

Right at the end of silence, as though she had been waiting for it, Rita asked me to remove the gold bracelet from her arm. Then she took it and fixed it onto mine, saying she wanted me to have it now, no telling what might get lost when she died. "Wear it in good health," she intoned, an expression adopted from our Jewish relatives on my father's side of the family. Although I meant for her to be wearing it in the coming years, I did not protest her warm generosity, understood she wanted to give me something she valued now.

I and Marianna, who had come down for the weekend, and Ruth, who had stayed overnight, picked apples down in the orchard this afternoon. (Marianna had adopted her birthname to replace "Bonnie" when she moved to the city, and started flourishing in her career as a serious artist.) By the time they had both left, I was tired and took a nap on a chaise on the deck, Rita knitting close by. After I awoke I asked how it felt to be in a houseful of Lesbians the evening before, which launched us into a difficult and sometimes painful wandering through her religion, our family history. . . .

She said she felt "alien" and "sad." She spoke carefully, sincerely. "Sad" because she saw all of us as women unaccepted by society, thus making our lives "hard, harder than even the normal person's, which is already hard enough."

She sounded to me as though she had spent the evening reading *The Well of Loneliness* instead of listening to all those women singing beautifully together, though she did agree the singing was beautiful.

She went on to say her sadness came also from her belief that we are in fact living lives of sin. "God did not intend for there to be Lesbians, so you are disobeying the will of God, and not returning to Him the love He is due." She labeled Lesbianism a sin like all the other sins, which she doesn't rank as bad or worse. "A sin is a sin," she declared, and named a couple of her own – jealousy, gossiping – as analogies. Then, as though to top off this list of depressing "facts," she asserted our relationships are "useless" because they do not make babies.

As she talked I tried to hear the feelings behind her words, the contradictions inherent in her beliefs. I worked at breathing deeply and was mostly successful at not rushing in to point out intellectual inconsistencies. I could see that all her beliefs hang together in a fragile interdependent network. If she questions one of them, they all come up to question. If she approved of Lesbianism, everything she has always believed about her God is suspect.

At one point, a non sequitur, she asked if I would ever come east to visit her if my sensitive ears could stand the travelling. I answered that I do have a wish to visit her new home, which I've never seen, and accompany her on her breakfast outings with her friends, whom she calls "the girls," do things for her around her house . . . but I worried that she would not be comfortable with me there, and explained I would not want to visit with the male relatives or welcome a concurrent visit from her son. At this last she was aghast: "Your own flesh and blood!" So I reminded her how he, four years older than I, had beat me up repeatedly when we were kids. She was shocked, disbelieving, wondering if over the years I have exaggerated. I was calm and steady, clear and insistent about what I know. She said she never knew, why hadn't I told her. And of course she did know, and I did tell her, but all I ever got from her was a tolerating: "Oh, you kids." As a child I had had to accept that she apparently thought his behavior was normal, nothing requiring her interference. Now she cried . . . and tried to fix it for herself, and me, by saying how he has changed, evidenced by how frequently he says his wife is beautiful. The worst of it is that now Rita probably thinks I am a Lesbian because my brother beat me; but the truth, as I came to understand it, was that he beat me precisely because I was a Lesbian, a "tomboy," and would never want or need his kind.

So my mother certainly has a low opinion of who I am, who my friends are, and thinks we are all sad because we "can't have children," the misfits/rejects of society. She listened to us sing at least fifty songs and came away feeling they all had "mournful tones."

Monday, September 23

I was up a little earlier than usual today, awakening from a beautiful dream in which I was a therapist for a child who had turned herself into a wasp-like insect, and I was helping her to choose her woman-self again. I was brilliant, totally intuitive. The child trusted me.

As we had planned, we were silent until supper, to give my ears a good long rest. I was glad to be inside myself, after the busy weekend, after yesterday's upsetting talk with Rita. During supper the three of us carried on mundane chit-chat, then cleared the table to play "Trivial Pursuit," a board game Bethroot bought for entertainment during Rita's visit. I worked on a sock I've been knitting as we took turns throwing the die and attempting to answer the questions on the cards. When I didn't know the answers, which happened more often than not, I invented funny ones, provoking laughter all around. And so we passed the evening in shallow silliness, accompanied by a thread of tension, laughing about trivia. I remembered all those times in my adolescence, thirty and more years ago, when laughter covered up a multitude of feelings in myself, in my mother.

Tuesday, September 24

(Morning:)

I have begun today feeling depressed about Rita, about her presence in my home, given what she thinks and feels about me and my friends. As I lay in bed stewing about it all, I got angry, with words like "stupid" and "ignorant" coming to mind. The anger alternated with a protective caring for myself and a compassion for the pain I trust Rita must feel, given what she believes about me while yet clearly wanting to love me.

I feel very alone this morning, having no woman's love close-in to tender me as I ride out this visit. I've had a nose-bleed; I cry . . . for Izetta's skillful help, for the loss of the fantasy that perhaps my mother would embrace who I am by embracing the woman-loving-woman in herself. I see this is completely unreal. I keep telling myself this visit is not over yet; I keep telling myself we are still in process, to stay open. But I don't really want someone in my home who is alienated from, saddened by, and in disagreement with what is at the core of my life, however gentle she is in expressing all that, however much pain her attitude ricochets back to her.

(Night:)

All day today I dragged myself around, crying most of the morning, uncomfortable around Rita, feeling withdrawn from her.

We drove down to South Myrtle Creek to get rocks to line a new flower bed and have a picnic lunch. I felt I was putting in time. When we returned, I went alone to the garden for about an hour and a half and spaded a new bed, turning over the hard-packed soil with muscle and determination. All the time I was working I thought about Sunday's conversation on the deck, and felt so disappointed in how things were going between my mother and me. At the same time, it was becoming clear I had to do something directly with Rita about my feelings, that I could not just shut her out and live with her yet another week. I'd have to talk with her and tell her what I was feeling, open myself to her. So I had a shower and joined her in the living room where she was stripping dried herbs from their stems, a task she had taken on in addition to the daily gathering of eggs in the henhouse.

I told her I was depressed from our talk, depressed to have her perspective about Lesbianism in my home. I explained that having her attitude/beliefs so up close was jarring to me, an undermining of the safety and peace I give to myself here in this isolated place. I have created in my home a sanctuary from the society that does not love or honor me, and here Lesbian-loving is the unqualified given. I wanted her to know it hurts when she says she loves me in spite of who I am, just because I am her daughter. I have determined in my life to be loved specifically because of who I am, and am so glad I am a Lesbian. I love being me.

It took a little while to get beyond our mutual slight defensiveness, but we did, and somehow we quickly got to more truthspeaking. In addition to "alien" and "sad" she said she had also felt comfortable and enjoyed herself at the sing, liked the conversations she had with individual women. But she has trouble with my Separatist attitude towards men, and the idea of Lesbian sex is beyond her understanding. And somehow we got from there to how often she hit me as a child, and from there to the time her father frightened me with his hands groping on my legs, and wet kisses on my lips, which he demanded I keep as "our secret." Whew! A lot off my chest, and a lot for her to take onto hers.

She wept at my description of her hitting me with her open hands, her fists, and sometimes with a wooden paddle – two inches wide and an inch thick – across my butt and the backs of my legs. She wept and assured me she does not remember any of this.

She was steeled rage at the information about her father whom she clearly hates but nonetheless gives daughterly attention to, as he languishes in a nursing home. "Why didn't you tell me about him?" she implored.

"Because I was afraid you wouldn't believe me, or else blame me somehow and be angry at me."

Appalled, she said that is what she'd read somewhere: how the child fears to tell the mother of such things. I told her I had figured out how to handle it myself, sat alone in the back seat of my grandfather's car when he drove me to choir practice, so he could not touch me.

She again brought up the subject of me visiting her, and again I said I worried she would be uncomfortable with my Lesbian self around her friends. "But it wouldn't come up," she offered, perhaps hopefully.

"Oh yes it would! It comes up! If your friends asked me anything about my life, my home, I would tell them as honestly and openly as I could. I *want* women to know there are women who intentionally make beautiful lives without men, and are proud to be Lesbians."

She thought quietly for a moment, continuing to strip the herbs, then slowly said, "Well, if you ever could come to visit, know you'd be welcome . . . and, well . . . whatever comes up, I'll just handle it."

My mother and I were running hurdles together. I helped her over each one as best I could, while staying with as much belief in, and love of, myself as these last years have helped me muster. The next one was her worry that I'll get AIDS, assuming I am a candidate for the homosexual statistics she reads about in her small-town newspaper. This one pushed me to the bottom of my resources. Her loving attention helped me clear the rung as I tearfully explained I am a Lesbian, a Separatist, have almost nothing to do with men, including homosexual men, that I don't use hypodermic needles, or have sex with strangers (or anyone else these days, for that matter!), and don't anticipate any blood transfusions. Indeed, she has as much chance of getting AIDS as I do.

It was a good talk, a deep and gentle talk. I worried the impact of it all might be too much for her, but she seemed steady, though I suspect she needed to cry more than she did. I wish now I had helped her to do that. She asked me pointedly, as she meticulously pulled the tiny thyme leaves from the stems, what I felt about her now, given all I had told her about my childhood, especially her hitting me. I replied that during those fifteen years when I had put the continent between us and wrote infrequently, I had felt the gamut of emotion, from rage to compassion. As I had become stronger in my love for my Lesbian self and developed a feminist knowing about the world of men's making, I had come to some understanding of her unhappiness and frustration as a wife and mother: she was angry in her life then, and hit me because she wanted to hit something, and I was available. She heard all this, was slow but candid in her agreement.

"But still," she persisted, "how do you feel about me now?"

I thought for a moment and spoke the growing truth: "When I look at you I do not see the angry mother who hit me. You are no longer that woman. You are this woman with a new life, and I feel warmth and opening with you. And I am no longer that little girl who is afraid of her mother's anger."

We looked steadily at each other then, two adult women each of whom had survived those sometimes awful years, and come together now to learn who we are.

At Rita's request, I had promised to make unsweetened hot apple pie for our dinner. As I was rolling out the dough, a feat I loved to watch my mother do when I was a child in her kitchen, she came up and put her arms around me, embracing me in a hug so soft and warm I was deeply grateful for all those hurdles we had just run together. As she walked away she said she felt sorry for "that little girl," meaning myself as a child. "I pity her," she said tearfully. And I knew she was feeling love for the child I was, wanting to scoop her up and comfort her.

"But y'know, she had spunk," I said with a chuckle. "She survived a lot, and grew up to be *me!*"

"How 'bout that!" Rita responded, her face beaming delight.

Our dinner was a re-creation of a scene that spunky girl loved, when she could have all the apple pie she wanted, fresh and steaming-hot from the oven, laced with milk. Rita and I each ate our fill, comforted and nourished by the pie and the caring deepening between us.

Wednesday, September 25

Bethroot and I were each up early for the drive up White Rock Road, and then the ever-more-arduous descent to the spring that spills into the old metal drum which feeds our water system. We cleaned a year's accumulation of leaves from the drum's screen, then removed it and shovelled out a thick layer of silt. After it had all been reassembled, Bethroot discovered a hole rusted out in the side of the drum. Ugh, that was hard to absorb, because of the big project repairing/replacing it would be. I plugged the hole as best I could with little sticks, and then we began the hike down the length of the mile-long waterline, an at-least-once-yearly event. As we went we opened drain plugs placed at long intervals to flush the line, checked for any damage to the pipe, and were glad to find none. We had taken our lunch along, but, because we moved so quickly through the forest, we saved it until we joined Rita at the house. Then we all drove back up to ultimately retrieve the car we had left, but first took a long drive up into the hills.

"My heavenly days, just look at that!" Rita exclaimed as each curve of the gravel road offered yet another breath-taking view of the miles and miles of ridges and expanse of sky. We stopped once where Pearly Everlasting grew generously on the shoulder of the road, where Rita picked a bouquet to dry and take back across the country with her.

I pointed out the approximate location of the spring box down at the bottom of the draw, and Rita was clearly impressed with the difficulty of our morning's work. She admired our ability to do the hard physical labor of the life here, but added a little motherly worry about it being too much for the two of us. She herself has worked hard all her life, still hangs her laundry out on a wash line all year around, so she knows and respects hard work. She clearly loves what our labor makes: the garden, the flower beds, a shed-full of firewood, shelves and shelves of canned food, my woodworking in the house. . . . She is a little in awe of my skills and I surmise she boasts proudly of me to her friends and relatives.

Thursday, September 26

Bethroot, Rita and I left here at 8:00 a.m. for a full day's outing, including several hours at Wildlife Safari in the morning. We had a grand time driving very slowly through the huge refuge where countless "wild" animals roam freely within a defined area of many acres. At one point we stopped to admire a white swan curled in sleep, when an emu startled us by nearly thrusting her head into the car before I hurriedly got the window closed! We laughed at the antics of monkeys cavorting on their moated island, were awe-struck by rhinos, camels, elephants, cheetahs . . . animals none of us had ever seen before except in pictures. The three of us were thrilled; sharing this experience made up for our somewhat forced pleasure with the trivia game three days ago.

Then on to town for a delicious lunch at a deli, followed by doing research at the Farm Co-op about a spring-box replacement, and lots of shopping. Rita, who made many skirts for me on her treadle sewing machine throughout my adolescence, helped me select some black satin material I'll use to make a lining for a wool coat a friend gave to me. We were hungry again by the time we had dinner at a Thai restaurant, and exhausted when we returned home. We all had a great time; Rita's enthusiasm was delightful.

Friday, September 27

Gotta get lots done today, projects piling up after the outings of these last two days. Though it is still morning, I am feeling tired, the ringing in my ears very loud now. My daily practice of meditation and Tai Chi, the mornings of silence, and writing in my journal have helped me be available for company all the rest of the day, but I am beginning to feel the accumulative effect of all these days of conversation.

Saturday, September 28

We went for a long walk in the forest, my mother and I. In my childhood, my mother's extended family gathered each Autumn for a picnic at Caledonia Park in the Pennsylvania mountains. After the feast we'd always take the easy hike on the path by the stream through the forest, ambling amidst the golds and oranges of the changing season. At the end of that path was the prize: a torrent of water falling down stone and concrete steps laid on the hillside for our pleasure. I loved those walks, those picnics, the mountain air, and fun with happy-for-the-day relatives.

Decades later, my mother and I walked in the evergreen forest of my hilltop home. The path was not so easy as the one we shared those years ago. Here there are brush and young trees reclaiming the crude roads made by the logging company even longer ago than those Pennsylvania walks. Rita found a sturdy stick to help her over fallen trees and through the thicket. We stopped often to rest, sat for a short while in a patch of sun on a gentle bank, each loving the forest and sky and earth surrounding us. We picked our way deeper into the forest until we came to the treasure I had wanted to show my mother: a large sinewy madrone reaching up past all the firs, touching sky with leaves, always shedding, always green, a great beautiful woman of a tree.

"Oh, how lovely," Rita spoke almost reverently, amazed, with me, at the curving smoothness of the bark that is more like skin, curling up each year and discarded for a new covering, snake-like and seemingly eternal.

As we retraced our steps Rita said she could hardly wait to tell her friends how she had walked this challenging forest path.

Sunday, September 29

Rita and I harvested the two remaining trees in the apple orchard this afternoon. I climbed the orchard ladder, filled the small bucket which I then handed down to my mother on the ground, she ready with another bucket for me to fill. We went around the trees, moving the ladder, filling up the boxes with this year's abundance. Rita stretched and picked apples within her reach, each one a testament to flexibility, each one a joyful reward. Up in the tree, I found a particularly exquisite, perfect red apple, polished it on my sleeve and handed it down to her saying, "This one is for my mother."

In a few days Rita will leave, our two weeks together at an end. I am liking her being here a lot and will be a little sad to see her go, because she has brought some warmth and caring into my life for these days. On the other hand, at dinner, when I mentioned my disappointment at not getting any letters from an old friend for so long now, Rita said sarcastically: "Yes! I remember having that experience with someone too." A dig. The first instance of this kind of energy since she came here. And so reminiscent of energy I remember from years ago. I winced. This was not the roly-poly seventy-year-old I've been enjoying. This was the woman who was my mother whom I did not love.

"Was that a dig?" I confronted, as gently and openly as I could.

"No, just an observation." She held her ground.

"It sounded like a dig to me."

Silence.

A very short exchange; a window into another reality. After time she might feel the right to make sarcastic comments, no longer focusing on a friendship between equals. After time she might take liberties, exercise what she would assume to be a mother's prerogatives. Strange she would do that. There has been kindness, care, and interest between us; we both said today how much we are enjoying each other. This was a throwback, a reminder to me to be careful, which makes me sad – I liked being able to forget about the mother of my adolescence and embrace Rita. I do understand that my distance from her for those fifteen years hurt her, but would she want me to remind her again why my letters were so few? Why I didn't want to see her all those years?

Monday, September 30

This evening the three of us took a picnic supper and the two dogs up to Red Top Spring, the small lake in the National Forest which begins just a few miles from home. The westering sun accented the countless shades of green and a touch of red and gold here and there, where vine maple or poison oak were obeying Autumn's call. The sandwiches, with tomatoes and cucumbers from the garden, and the cookies I baked this afternoon, all tasted especially good in the cool mountain air.

Lady had difficulty getting comfortable on the drive and then almost fell into the water as she struggled to get a drink on the steep bank. When it became apparent her legs were too weak for her to be able to maneuver the slope, Bethroot and I went to her rescue. Dear sweet Lady, I wonder what I will yet learn through her.

As we drove back down from the lake, Bethroot asked Rita about my father's death, and Rita spoke the story. I leaned up to her from the back seat, touched her arm, focused on this woman's experience of death as her culture rules it, gave her my caring attention. With moistened eyes, she finished the story at the gate. I caressed her cheek with my palm and said gently: "That was a hard time for you." Then I got out to open the gate.

She is easy to be kind to, feel warm towards. Except when she lapses into a former identity, like on the deck at lunch today. Bethroot had asked Rita how she got such strong thick wrists, in contrast to the small ones both Bethroot and I have. Rita made a fist and joked about how she got them from beating her kids. I did not fall to the bottom like I did two years ago when she made the same joke, but I said very seriously that that was not funny. Rita agreed it wasn't, but I don't know how deep her agreement went. Maybe a part of her does remember, and her anger rises up and defends the striking-out she did at her children, when mothering was so often angering for her. I think she does open to those memories sometimes, and doesn't know what to do with them, how to heal from them. We were talking earlier about dreams, and she shared she sometimes dreams about my father: "bad dreams," full of her anger. She said she doesn't like those dreams, does not want to feel that way anymore. I talked about our dreams being one place where we work on our material, especially if we're not working on it in our waking life. I see this jolly gentle woman hides a well of anger. She carries resentment in her body which she says got heavier and heavier with the births of each of her three children. In many ways she is happier now, her children all in homes of their own, her husband dead. She loves having a home of her own, not having to clean up after or take care of anyone, having control over everything she does. And she is sometimes lonely too.

·

Tuesday, October 1

This morning I finished putting the bottom on a new large flower box for the end of the trailer, while Rita sat nearby, crocheting a cap for me and watching me work. I welcomed her opinion about the number of drainholes I should drill, and her good suggestion that I line the box with plastic sheeting. We had a

leisurely lunch, each took a short nap, then drove down the road
and parked at the gate. From there we walked across the county
road and then on down to South Myrtle Creek where we sat on
the rocks. We enjoyed the scene, the water low yet in the creek
bed, enjoyed the easy companionship we could give to each other.
Rita removed her shoes and socks and got her feet wet with the
cold mountain water. I remembered her doing the same thing when
we would stop at the Narrows on my way home from a Summer
week of happiness at Camp Nawakwa. That creek stop was a
helpful transition for me then, giving me a little more of the taste
of camp before I was trapped for another year with my brother's
bullying and my mother's anger.

The creek rock was too hard to sit on for Rita's fragile back, as
was the dirt bank back up at the gate, where we watched a
butterfly work the wild clover. On her last day here, after two
weeks of trouble-free living in the woods, without an indoor
bathroom, walking on steep hills and through the forest, on the
last day Rita's back began to hurt. This was frightening to her,
because the pain can become extremely severe and only an
immediate trip to her chiropractor and total rest alleviates it. I
know a lift to alleviate back pain and convinced Rita to let me do
it for her. I planted my feet wide, stood with my back to her belly,
her arms stretched over my shoulders. Slowly I bent at my hips
and pulled Rita's relaxed weight onto my back and hips, balancing
the weight and passing it through my legs into the solid earth. We
each breathed deeply as I stood holding her that way for several
minutes, her body stretching over the curve of mine. Then she
slowly slid from my back as I straightened myself up. When asked,
she said the lift had given her some relief. I was concerned and
attentive the rest of the day, though not able to gauge the extent
of her discomfort, or know with certainty if she was tending herself
well enough. By bedtime she was quite uncomfortable, should not
have sat up on the couch all evening looking at my photograph
albums. When she was ready to turn in she asked if I had any

Vicks VapoRub. I got it from the medicine cabinet and offered to give her a massage after she got in bed.

And so I rubbed my mother's back, my strong hands and fingers kneading the tight muscles, tendering the pain. She loved it, was so grateful for my touch, the healing in my hands, the kind of attention that is absent in her life. The pungent odor of the salve filled the little room and carried me to memories of my childhood, to the times when I had a cold and my mother would come to my bed at night and rub my chest with Vicks. I remember the odor filling my nose, stinging my eyes a little, making me have to close them; I remember Rita's strong hands rubbing my chest, the salve easing my breathing. On those occasions I felt healing, loving attention from my mother; I felt like a cared-for child and I could bask in sweet mothering energy.

Over three decades later I rub my mother's hurting back, mothering her, daughtering her, easing her pain.

Wednesday, October 2

The long drive down to the airport was pleasant, the day sunny and beautiful as all these two weeks have been. Chatting away, I missed the airport exit, costing us another five minutes, though we still had plenty of time to check Rita's luggage and have breakfast, to which she treated me, in the airport restaurant. We both ordered pancakes: gummy white flour, but tasty, especially with the sour cream I generously applied.

Rita was nervous about the day of flying, and a little tearful of leaving me. After we had finished eating she reached across the table and took my hand to tell me: ". . . in case something happens and we don't see each other again, well . . . God bless you . . . take good care of yourself . . . have a happy life . . . I love you."

I had already rushed in with self-conscious banter before she spoke her last three words. I said, "Well, in case something happens and we don't see each other again, you have a helluva time on the way out!" I did mean it – I want her to have all the happiness and joy possible as she lives out her life. But I knew she wanted to hear "I love you, Mother."

We held hands sitting together in the passenger departure area, then I walked her to the exit when the call came to board. We waved goodbye as she left the building, then again when she reached the top of the stairway, before she disappeared into the body of the airplane. I stayed and stared out the window until the plane left the gate area, until the tears came, sorry I could not tell her that I loved her, sorry that, since my mate left, and my animal companions died, those words do not flow easily from me. Rita was right to see sadness, the mournfulness in me, the set of my mouth which she called grim. But I am content she also saw the beauty of my life, the beauty of what I make, the Madrone I have become.

When I had finished my writing, the wren awoke and grew a little restless in my hand. I took her downstairs and back outside where I lay my hand on the walkway, my mother's gold bracelet hanging loosely from my wrist. The little bird stepped gingerly from my palm and flew off into the forest.

Autumn

The early morning air
greets me with a snap
when I leave my quilted bed
dress
and go outside
jacketed and capped
to pee on thirsty ground
and feed the hens.

Purple, magenta, red petunias
on the deck
tended earnestly
through summer's drought
begin to lose our gamble
to the cold nights,
are beckoned to browning
and decay.
Zinnias, cosmos, marigolds
already succumbed to an early frost
in the lower garden,
become a testament to mortality,
their bright colors all but gone,
the flowers stunned
atop their stems
by Autumn's surprise.

The chickens know my rising,
come running from the hill

where they've scratched and pecked
since dawn,
looking for handouts
left by a starry night.
I call a loud "chee-chick!"
fill the kettle with grain
to spread around the coop
for the clucking flock.
With ever-shortening light
the ones still young enough to lay
leave fewer and fewer eggs
for my gathering.

The grey goose
often comes to call the hens with me,
her loud honking
announcing breakfast,
expecting the filling of her bowl.
This morning she is late,
and I wonder . . .
has October's grey chill
pulled her to a southern clime,
though she has lived here since a gosling?
Soon I see her big white belly
and three-foot span of wings
soaring twenty feet above the lane.
Her body claims the air with grace,
asserts her proud capacity for flight,
the memory of migration
she carries in her genes.
The goose glides toward me,
backwings a landing near her waiting bowl,
and chooses home again.

Today I think to set a fire
to warm my hearth,
and fill the firewood bin.

January Felling

I had begun the day in tears, sadness lingering from the latest exchange of difficult letters with Izetta, whom I hadn't seen for almost two years. The creak of the rocker was soothing as I felt the aching and confusion stirred up again. Bethroot and I had arranged for JP to come fell some trees with us that day, and I was glad when she arrived shortly after noon, at the end of our daily keeping silent, glad for an afternoon of vigorous work to absorb my focus and energy.

Evergreen forest covers most of the forty acres of our hilltop home, with clearings here and there: a grassy knoll where I am blessed with grand dramatic sunsets, a large terraced amphitheater of a garden below the house, and beyond that the small apple orchard in the draw just before the forest begins again. Between the house and the orchard the hill slopes southward, the sun often warming the house even in the Winter, when on many days fog covers the valley far below. The prior year we had felled one large fir, a cedar, and a few small madrones on this hillside, wanting to open the space to the view of the distant southern ridges. But the remaining trees grew steadily toward the horizon, reaching for the sky, filling in the airy spaces between them.

JP studied the huge fir that had been assumed to be the northeast corner of the new six foot high garden fence, built several years ago by the four of us who homed here together then. The top east-west wall of fencing never did get as far as this tree, the old fence still standing on the rotting posts, still barring hens, deer and dogs from the garden which feeds us year-round. About four years before, I had watched my lover climb high into this tree and saw off the big lower branches one-by-one as she descended, removing the limb-rungs of her ladder as she came. Then we could see more of the colorful garden from the house, and some sky below the yet majestic top of the tree. But that majesty had grown taller and fuller in these years and I yearned to see the open sky through the windows.

For many months I had been in conversation with the spirit of this tree, imploring her safely down. I understood the enormity of my intention, as enormous as the tree herself. Recently there had been a fierce windstorm that pulled down many of the dead madrones up the hill in the government-owned forest. I watched nervously as this big fir near the house bent and swayed with each howling gust. She looked too vulnerable in her top-heavy shape, with no tall sister trees close by to cut the force of the wind.

I sensed from JP's careful scrutiny that she was rather intimidated by the size of this would-be "garden post," at least twenty-two inches in diameter where the cuts should be made, a few feet up from the base. Though she had more experience than I in felling trees, this would be the largest she ever attempted. I understood her nervousness, encouraged her to proceed at a gentle pace. A light rain fell as we made our way through the thick brush down the hill to scout the path the tall tree would need to fill, and to look at another fir near the orchard we would want to cut if there were time and energy, and yet another, a cedar, who although not yet filling much of the sky, surely would in the near future. Better to cut her down now, as well as the young madrone in the big fir's path, than wait until her size became more difficult to cut and place.

It is an awesome act to cut down a tree, big or little, though the big ones, the ones who tower over me like giant goddesses, the ones who have lived on this land long before I came here, these big trees are part of the character of the land herself, holding in their massive trunks the story of the land, the years passing, the changes in the weather, season to season. They have watched us work and build, play and love; they have listened as well to our rage, and to our wailing grief. The trees hold me many days when my spirit wants to slip away; they wave me to renewal. In their strength and perseverance I am reminded of my own. I approach their felling with reverence and respect.

We began with the young madrone, who had divided herself into two sister trunks at an early age. Her olive-brown womanly skin glistened from the rain, her muscular curving twin bodies . . . a stilled dance. A chorus of madrones stood well behind her to the east, a grove that will grow tall and wide to my welcome in the years to come. The twins fell easily, making it safer to fell the big fir farther up the hill. We returned there, checked the fuel and oil level in the chainsaw, then placed at a safe distance the wedges and hammer which might be needed, the tools for the saw, extra gas and oil.

We three stood with the fir and oriented ourselves, planned carefully the placement of the two hinge cuts, the angle of the fall. While there was little chance of the tree falling anywhere but downhill, and thus safely far from our beloved house, it was essential she not hit the beehives on the left, and preferable that she miss the garden fence on the right. I wore a snug headset to protect my hypersensitive ears from the din of the saw. Bethroot had hers on too, and I had given a pair to JP to wear, though I was disturbed to see she was unused to it, preferring to be able to hear and read the saw's noise and any other sounds she didn't want to miss.

Bethroot positioned herself several yards opposite the intended direction of the fall, while I stood off to the left, perpendicular to the cut, and kept my eyes on the top of the tree as JP entered the trunk with the saw. Twice during the two hinge cuts, for making the large notch which would guide the tree's descent, the chain jumped off the bar; twice we had to go inside to my workbench where I filed the burred edges of the chain guides. But all went well with the third and final back cut, though the tree stood stately resting on the relatively thin wall of the hinge. I stood through all the sawing with my palms upraised to the tree, asking for her life, thanking her for giving me the sky, promising her I would honor her by using her substance for firewood, borders for new flower beds, log mulch to protect shrubs from the hens' scratching, her stump a table for bird seed.

I had learned many years earlier, at my first felling, that trees do not come suddenly or quickly crashing to the ground. It took many strikes on the big metal wedge placed in the back cut to coax the tree down, each blow reverberating up the trunk and out to the tip of each branch, an internal ballet of cellular communication. A sharp crack announced the beginning of her slow and graceful falling. The thirty feet of branches at the top of the tree whooshed through the air like the wing feathers of a giant bird; the great weight of her limbless trunk hit the earth with a deep thud, landing just as we had asked of her, missing both the hives and the fence. JP glowed with well-deserved pride, and much relief, as Bethroot and I rejoined her at the stump. With joyful gratitude I stroked the thick bark of the great tree lying on the hillside, quietly honoring the goddess in her, the goddess in me, the cycles of change, of living and dying, that embrace us both.

The afternoon was not yet half gone, there would be enough light, and we had enough good spirits and energy to continue on down the hillside to the fir just at the top of the orchard. The big low-hanging limbs of this tree had spread wide, making a shady spot to rest when we would slowly run the rototiller from the barn to the garden in the Spring, then back to the barn again at gardening season's end. The tiller is mostly in retirement now, since we have changed to a permanent mulching system in the garden, and those big limbs, as well as the tree's height, have grown to eat the view of the orchard and devour the skyline of the distant ridges. We repeated our procedure: JP doing the cutting, while Bethroot spotted from behind and uphill, and I off to the side. Again with upraised hands I watched the top of the tree, dark green against the pale grey sky, and yelled announcement at the first sign of falling. This fir, and then the cedar back up the hill below the hives, came down without mishap, rewarding our caring and careful labor and attention. The three of us had worked well together, and we were pleased with what had been accomplished, a testament of our Lesbian friendship and the bond between our country homes as we shared our skills.

It had rained lightly during the hours of our work so we were all a little wet and chilled before we made ourselves comfortable in the house, grateful for the warm woodstove and hot herbal tea. Vegetable stew had simmered all afternoon; I mixed up a batch of biscuits. While they baked I stood at the window looking at the fallen trees it would take me several days to cut and split to firewood; I stared down at the orchard and at the wide expanse of sky. The view had been completely changed; the horizon had jumped miles further away. There was a sense of new, clear space, an invitation. I remembered my tears and aching of the morning and hoped for the possibility in me of new horizons, of new undefined space in which to become yet more of who I could be, like the infant daughter trees who dot the hillside and will want to grow like their mothers to claim the sky.

The biscuits came swollen and hot from the oven. I called the others to the table, and as I took my seat I glanced again at the orchard and smiled to realize that, come Spring, for the first time from this window, I will see the apple trees in bloom.

Self-Sculpture

Tucked in the smallest of the borrowed tins a friend returned, via UPS, was a small bag of four homemade cookies. How thoughtful: she must have made a batch of cookies and put some in the tin for a smile. After lunch I gobbled three of them. Bethroot had just a nibble, found the sugary peanut butter not to her taste. I could have eaten the fourth quite easily, but thought I'd save the last one for another time.

Bethroot left soon thereafter, gone for the weekend. As soon as I was alone on the land, I settled gladly into solitude, and returned to sculpting the arm of madrone on my workbench. This was the third madrone sculpture I had done that Winter. The first was a bannister for the back steps, an improvement suggested by my mother; the second a staff I made for Bethroot, which quickly became a prop for her latest theater piece; and now this strange specimen I had found when cutting firewood from the slashpile left by neighbors' logging along the road the prior year. I had seen an amazonal arm in the wood, bent at the elbow, flexed and muscular, the skin stretched taut beneath hard, dried bark. For many days I had been painstakingly removing that bark with the small blade of a carving tool, watching the veins of the wood emerge as the roughness fell away, a meditation on fine detail, a labor of love.

I had been working maybe twenty minutes when I realized I was feeling somewhat light-headed, like a cannabis high. This was curious: I seldom smoked anymore, but had intentions of doing so later, when I finished at the workbench and would go for a walk to initiate my rare weekend alone. A few more minutes passed and the high intensified. Puzzled, I could not imagine why this was happening to me. And then I remembered: my friend's cookies. Of course. If I had remembered her proclivities, as she surely must have assumed I would, I would not have eaten three of them! But I chuckled with delight, glad for the medicine to come into my body as food rather than smoke.

I continued to work on the madrone, guided by the light from the skylight. Following the natural curve of the wood, the graceful line of the grain, I labored with a concentration that was complete, an absorption in the work that became a passageway into the wood itself. As I scraped and sanded, I slowly realized I had been addressing myself as I sculpted the bannister, the staff, and now this angled arm, attending my own body, loving myself with my hands, my growing skill.

When the light became too dim at the workbench, it was time to go outside, while there was still comfort in the warmish day. I banked the woodstove, then Ladydog and I strolled through the garden and down to the orchard, where I wanted to see the newly-opened view from there up to the house, now that the two large firs and a cedar had been cut from the hillside. What I saw was as grand as I had anticipated. Our temple of a house stood elegantly rustic among the evergreens, the forest lifting upward behind her roundness like a crown. Amazed that all this beauty was my home, I understood full well again my being planted here, as certainly as the young madrones standing together below the house.

The Winter sky darkened further and I needed to be up out of the shadowed draw, needed to be at a higher place where there would be more light. Lady laboriously pulled herself up from where she had sat waiting for me, and we walked in leisurely tandem on the deer path to the barn. From there we'd take the easiest way back up the hill. At the barn I paused to look back at the orchard and the terraced garden beyond, while Lady went to drink from the water trickling out of the end of "Black Snake Creek," our plastic waterline which ends at the barnyard. As she drank, she was unable to keep her balance on the slope, and her aging legs collapsed under her. I helped her up when her thirst was satisfied.

We slowly made our way back up to the house and then on out the lane and up the mowed path to the grassy knoll overlooking the layers of ridges to the east and south. There I stood and stretched, pushing my leg muscles to the limit of their elasticity, flexed my thighs to summon the strong sinewy madrones hidden beneath the soft fullness that is my mother's legacy. Twisting at my waist, I fingered the air as my outstretched arms pulled my shoulders spiralling from my swollen menopausal belly. Around to the left . . . around to the right . . . slowly back and forth, and back again, my eyes scanning the full circle of the hilltop. Lady watched me with quietly intent curiosity. Then I stopped stretching, squatted, and watched her, the beauty of her, her blondes and reddish-browns, her snowy white chest and black ear tips ethereal in the fading light. We held each other's gaze while clouds parted briefly now and then for the moon to show a hazy half-faced glow. I stood, and ambled back to the warm house, the big dog keeping on at my side.

I lit one lamp as Lady stiffly settled herself onto her bed, then I went out onto the deck. Moonlight was pale on the draw down to the orchard and the valley below, the ridges pillowed by the cloudy sky. I lounged deeply in a roomy canvas chair and let the subtle motion of the clouds, the changing character of the evening sky, lull me with peaceful simplicity. Only my legs marked the passing of the time: after what must have been nearly an hour, a chill crept up my calves and I wanted motion again. I bid goodnight to the moon and returned to the warmth of the house.

Because I was alone on the land, I decided to light all the kerosene lamps just for me, give myself the grandeur of all twelve walls, bring light to all the space, call the shapes and rich colors to my singular pleasure. As I lit the seventeenth, and last, one, I placed it on the workbench and worked once more with the madrone, enticed by the color of the woodgrain kissed by yellow lamplight. Using finer and finer grades of sandpaper, and then an oiled cloth, and finally my bare hands, I rubbed the wood to a rich brown patina. With my fingers I stroked the wooden wrinkles of the inner curve of the elbow; my palms massaged the ligneous flesh.

When I tired at the workbench I stepped into the inner circle, carefully pulled the altar to one side, and lay on the thick carpet. Lady was still asleep on her bed, no cats around. Silence. Solitude gave me permission to fill the space, first with long slow stretches, then on my feet with round after round of even slower, finely measured Tai Chi. With each sequence my balance became more certain, my concentration sure; I grew so intimate with the form that I began to improvise, explored movements to mirror the strength and fluidity of the madrones, both the piece on my workbench and the grove on the hillside.

The windows had long since blackened with the deepening night by the time I ate a bowl of vegetable stew. I gave Ladydog her supper and saw her back to her bed, where she groaned as she carefully lowered the burden of her weight. I gently stroked the silky length of her, whisper-sang her name, then made the round of the house to blow out all the lamps. My legs were weary as I climbed the staircase to my bedroom, where my clothes fell to the floor as I undressed. Naked on the high bed, my skin reflected the yellow glow from one lamp on the sill. My hands moved to my inner thighs, slackened muscles yielded to the kneading of my palms; my fingers reached to the moist folds of my long neglected lips, the swollen knot. I made exquisite love to myself, with a focus that again lacked nothing, with an absorption in the moment that became a passageway into myself, coming to deep moaning orgasm for the first time in several months. With my last energy I put on my pajamas, then pulled up the flannel sheet and thick quilt, and blew out the lamp. Sleep covered me softly.

Mid-Spring Snow

Snow! in May!
A comedy of white
The hens confused
waiting for their grain
My spirit tickled
a chuckle prodded loose
its rarity matched
by the oddity of snow

So *laugh!*
the snow commands
My chest opens to obey
squeezes out a titter
                a giggle
                        a guffaw

Lila, trickster goddess
sends me snow in May
teases me to smile
conspires to make me laugh,
and grins her satisfaction.
The snow a psychic rainbow
a promise this long flood of woe
will end
that mirth will come again.

Caves
a Summer's Story

What a joy it was when Sami Slate's black furry belly began to suggest she was pregnant. There had been so many losses of animal friends of late, most recently Hera, the dowager Bantam hen already in residence when I arrived ten years before. As one vacant space after another appeared in my life, my chest got to feeling like an empty, drafty cavern, where once it had been filled with the bond I had with Phyrste, and the coupling I made with Izetta. I worked hard to heal from the break-up, immersed myself in my work, my home, relative solitude, the silence of the land. But all my pain and disappointment lay just beneath the surface, easily set astir when something reminded me of the depth, the passion, the gaiety of that mating . . . as well as its anguish.

Bethroot felt all these losses too, as well as some particularly her own. The two of us pulled ourselves through our grievings, trusting as much as we each could in a happier future. So when one of our two nine-year-old cats promised birth, babies, new life, there was cause for joy!

Not knowing exactly when Sami must have had an encounter with a stray and this pregnancy began, her belly still only somewhat swollen, I was surprised when she suddenly became quite upset one Wednesday evening late in July. She mewed repeatedly, wanted nonstop stroking. I supposed she must be ready to give birth, even though she was not yet looking as enormous as I had expected. Sami followed me to my bedroom, where I had prepared a box for the delivery and first nest for a litter. Bethroot joined us after finishing supper clean-up, and for the next couple of hours she and I took turns humming a soothing lullaby and gently rubbing Sami's small but tight black belly. She meowed her complaint, cried for our total focus when Bethroot turned away to light a kerosene lamp, and then again when I changed into my pajamas. Finally, the hour grown quite late and Sami eventually less agitated, more her normal self, Bethroot left for her yurt bedroom up the hill. Sami left too, but then came back to me for more attention. She came and went most of the night, mewing all the while, waking me frequently. It was not until daybreak that she snuggled in beside me and we both slept soundly until after 8:00. I didn't know what all her restlessness had been about, but apparently we had weathered some crisis and Sami cuddled on my lap as usual while I had my morning tea. When she heard Bethroot arrive at the trailer porch, she bounded up there for breakfast.

Bethroot left for two days in Eugene and the day passed uneventfully, but then came another restless night, with Sami mewing while I, heavy-eyed, petted her continuously. Around 3:00 a.m. there came a different sort of cry, a meow-become-a-howl, like I remembered Missy Moonshine making when she gave birth to Sami, Lillith One, and their litter mates. I lit two kerosene lamps, took the cloth from the box and laid it out on my bed and got Sami and myself situated for labor and birth. Over the next three and a half hours I kept watch as Sami's belly alternately contracted and relaxed; pink fluid discharged from her vagina, which she cleaned up immediately. All this while she lay as close to me as she could possibly get, curled against my breast, under my arm. My body felt like an extension of hers as I gently massaged the flesh beneath her soft fur for all those hours, and she in turn washed my face and head. We shared an intimacy we each trusted, an intimacy poignant enough to conjure keen recollection of another. As Sami and I lay pressed together in the dream-deep night, I dozed in and out of memories, sensations.

I kissed her lips, I tongued her mouth, I sniffed her nostrils, I rubbed cheeks with her. I pulled her toward me, my mind sucked at her.

I wanted into her womb. I wanted to grow in her, fill her up, be life growing in her. I wanted to be my babyself in her, becoming woman. Swelling her. She would carry me, her body would carry me. She the planet, the universe. I wanted into her womb.

We made love, we planted the garden, we made love; we made covers for the strawberry beds, we hiked to the upper forest and made love; we climbed the ladder to the house roof to clean the chimney and sang full-voiced to the distant ridges.

We made love.

I handled her according to my instincts, led by my desire for her, my passion to cover and fill her body with my own. She handled me with a passion new to her, called from me my womanhood, balanced me on her fingertips while I filled the valley with my fertile howl.

By 6:30 in the morning the contractions stopped, and there were no babies. While there was a lull in the drama, I decided I had better go feed the hens. I had to carry Sami with me while I accomplished this task because there was no way she was going to let me go off without her. For all I knew her babies were about to pop out, so I carried her in the birthing cloth while I cast grain to the hens in their yard.

In the next two hours there were no further contractions but she mewed constantly, was very agitated and restless. I speculated she might be pleading for an early meal so I gave her the usual canned fare, which she devoured ravenously. Then back to bed with hopes for either some rest or an actual birth, but Sami remained disquieted. So then I made her a scrambled egg, which she also gobbled up. And then more canned food when I fed Lillith One and always-hungry plump Mailava at the trailer. She continued to cry, but after a while settled on my lap and purred. I really did not know what to make of it all. I didn't remember Ki-Ki, the city cat I had twenty years before, or Missy Moonshine going through all this, taking so long, being so upset. I worried that if all that fluid in the night was from broken placentas, then maybe the babies would die, perhaps were dead already. I felt so ignorant about what is such a natural process, and frustrated by the old thievery which had robbed my ancestors of their women's ways of knowing, leaving me a poor inheritance. But I would be with Sami for whatever happened and at the moment she was content on my lap, looking at me dreamily. Ha! That contentedness lasted only a few minutes before she was down, and back, and gone again. I had to let go of knowing anything, of having any sense of control.

I proceeded with my usual morning routine, all to the constant accompaniment of Sami's distressed crying. I thought maybe meditating in the inner circle would help us both. She did settle on my thigh for a bit, but was soon crying again, and proceeded to pace back and forth between the cat door and me. I continued to meditate, counting on a source of peace inside myself to guide us both. Sami appeared to know so little of what she was doing, as though her body was as much a mystery to her as it was being to me. Then I tried a vocal meditation, hoping the vibrating tones would be soothing. While Sami continued to pace and scold, I placed the vowel sounds in my womb, my chest, my throat. Just as I was about to resonate the short *i* in the space between my ears, I suddenly understood all the yelling Sami was doing was asking me to go somewhere with her. Earlier, after her third breakfast, she had started up the path behind the trailer to the old coldframe, but came back down at my urging and I had carried her back to the house. Now I got up quickly and told her I'd follow her. She immediately understood and led me out of the house and up to that path.

Past the coldframe we crossed a small clearing and then the path, cat-size, turned into the forest. Pushing myself through brush Sami could walk easily beneath, I followed her to an ancient rotting stump, pieces of it fallen flat, the whole thing hanging at an angle. Sami disappeared around to the other side and into the belly of the stump. I climbed around in cautious pursuit and discovered a small cave, barely eight inches from floor to ceiling. After carefully pulling aside the debris of one section of a small wall, I could see Sami Slate's black velvet body crouched inside. Her desperate mewing had stopped. She had transformed from a panicked domestic to a serene and knowing creature of the forest. I worked at settling myself as best I could in the brush, pulled up my sweatshirt hood to protect my neck and head from mosquitoes. I sat in silence, content to study the forest around me and admire the landscaping I had been doing in recent years on the hillside down beside the house, the hard physical labor carrying me through recurring bouts of depression. Huge pink lilies blooming in a bed they shared with earlier irises and later gladioli inspired a melody, so I began to sing. A growl came from the cave. I stopped singing and looked around, saw nothing threatening about, and took up the song again. Another growl. I looked in at Sami: her chartreuse eyes instructed me to keep silent, not call attention to our presence: the growl had been for me. I apologized and, since I was exhausted from too little solid sleep, it seemed like a good time for a nap, so curled up on a bed of dry madrone leaves, blackberry vines and poison oak sticks, with my head close to the cave opening in case anything new happened. With my handkerchief covering my face, I breathed the bittersweet odor of the chamomile flowers I had picked the day before, when I used the handkerchief as a basket.

I lay there quite uncomfortably for a half hour or so, unable to sleep, though my eyes begged for it. Deciding food might help where sleep was wanting, I told Sami I was going to the house for a while and would be back. Taking a more woman-size route, I made my way down to where Mailava was patiently waiting, heeding my earlier request that she not come into the forest. Although Sami was on good terms with the dogs, I knew she did not want them spying out her nest.

I took care of the essentials: breakfasted quickly, watered the thirsty flower boxes on the deck, fed Ladydog at her place in the house, let the hens out of their yard for their day of free-ranging, and collected the eggs. I gathered snack food for later, and a book, and returned to Sami's lair, a little concerned not to see her at the opening when I arrived. I set aside my things and stretched to peer inside; when my eyes adjusted to the darkness I saw Sami's black body far back in the near-black cave, apparently taking precaution lest the racket of my approach signaled another animal than myself. She came forward when I spoke to her.

I had hoped being in her hidden place would be the catalyst to bring on the contractions and the births, but nothing of that sort was happening so far as I could tell. Sami seemed at peace and closed her eyes often as though napping. I reconciled myself to reading, later munched on an apple and trail mix, all of which made me even more drowsy, so I lay down and was able to doze off and on, occasionally looking in at Sami who seemed to be enacting the same rhythm. After about an hour of this I really wanted a proper nap and announced I was going to the house. When I got there I called Sami once, wishing her nearby, but I would honor her choice of where she wanted to be. She soon came trotting in and joined me on the couch, lay on my chest. We both were quiet and restful for a while, but then the mewing started again. I went upstairs to the bed and cloth; she followed, her mouth open, panting. There was more fluid coming from her vagina, which she quickly cleaned. As she had during the night, she thoroughly washed herself, as well as my face when I was near. I rubbed her belly, stroked her back and head, but nothing I did seemed to help. She jumped down from the bed and headed toward the staircase. I suspected she wanted to go back to the forest and I wept with frustration and worry. The babies I thought I had felt moving in her belly during the long night showed no movement now. At her loud insistence, I wearily followed her back to the cave, where she lay content, eyes and mouth closed.

I stayed at the stump-cave until dinner time, watched Sami make herself comfortable in the various rooms of her secret den. She rested peacefully, made no sound the whole afternoon. I explained to her I was returning to the house, would come back to see her later if she chose not to come. By the time I got to the house, she came sprinting down the hill, though I had not called her this time. I fed her vigorous appetite before making my salad, then ate and knitted on the couch while Sami slept on my lap, the evening passing quietly.

I had gotten up to make a cup of tea when Lillith One came in. I was glad for the opportunity to hold her for a while, wanting to give her some attention after three days of being so focused on Sami, who was displeased enough with my regard given elsewhere that I feared a quarrel between the cats. In the end I had both the black Sami and the black-spotted, white Lillith tolerating each other on my lap, as I tried to knit over their heads. Around 9:00 Sami started to have contractions again. I put her and Lillith down, went outside to pee, then hurried to my bed where Sami and I could concentrate on what was happening in her body. But she didn't come up with me then, nor later, after I had read for an hour or so, or even when, against my better judgment, I went outside to call her. When she did not immediately appear, I stopped calling. Although I wanted her with me, I had to accept she was where she belonged.

Sami never did join me that night, so I slept undisturbed and felt fairly rested when I got up the next morning. I fed the hens, then went to check on things at the cave. I could hear Sami growl as I arrived. She was in yet a different part of the structure, where she looked comfortable and content, all curled up but watchful. I wondered what had happened during the night, what story her body held. Were there babies in that cave or was Sami's belly still carrying the weight of them, alive or dead?

When I visited her a second time later in the morning, she had curled in a different position; I had to squeeze my face slightly into an opening of the cave in order to see her. I spoke lovingly to her as she looked at me with cautious eyes. Her breathing was slow and regular, but one small part of her black fur seemed to be breathing at a much faster rate. I stared at that part for several minutes until it moved apparently independently of the rest of Sami's body! Soon I could see a teeny black tail curl up around a teeny black body. So Sami had birthed at last. My relief and hurrah were respectfully silent.

She came down for breakfast later when Bethroot dished out the cat food, as is her morning routine. Bethroot didn't know about the cave or the kitten, having returned from her trip very late the night before, long after I was asleep. Staying silent, which was our morning custom, I wrote her a note to follow me after Sami had finished eating. Though the new mother lingered behind in the sun for a few moments, she appeared at the cave when we did. We had time to see the one little black kitten lying inside, just before Sami entered and enveloped the tiny body with the softness of her own. There she stayed, apparently all afternoon, as Bethroot and I went about the farm work. It was very satisfying to cull a superabundance of weeds from the garden, and then load the pickup with firewood, seasoned by the elements for a year. And I finally cleaned the screen in the dirt trap in the waterline. Just before my suppertime I took food and water to a grateful Sami. She moved away from the baby slightly so I could easily touch it. Sami was on the alert, but welcomed my scratching her ears. Then I picked up the little one who protested with a hearty one-day-old kitten scream. I glanced quickly under the tail, long enough to see we had a daughter.

The next evening, when I carried up her supper, I found that Sami had moved to the outer, separate chamber of the cave complex, the hole beneath the leaning stump itself, the walls charred black from some ancient cause. She ate calmly, then came out for a stretch, her baby safely tucked within. Sami extended her front paws to my thighs, looked into my eyes with the love we share. I stroked her, tickled her ears as she purred. The baby started to fuss, so Sami returned to curl in the hole, cooing to the kitten's complaint until a breast was found. I placed fresh water at the mouth of the cave and bid Sami goodnight. I missed her as I returned to the house, had gotten to feeling so close to her during those long nights of labor on my bed. She was one of the creatures in my life who made me feel a part of the nature of things. When she curled up close to me at night I felt the two of us kin to the multitudes of other animals secreted on this isolated hill.

I visited the cave several times during the next two days, spaced between farm chores and visitors, including a friend who came one morning to give me the massage promised since my early March birthday.

I lie face down on a soft sheet on the thick-foamed table, set up between Lady's bed on one side and the woodbin on the other. The oiled hands are big and certain as they knead and stroke my body. I relax, yield my limbs, my muscles to be read by fingers, palms. My skin welcomes the sweet-smelling oil.

I lie in the silence of my home, broken only by the sound of my deep breathing, and involuntary groans as tight muscles are found . . . and surrender. I lie inert, passive, let myself be moved by the pushing on my back, the lifting of an arm, a leg, as I sink deeper and deeper into the universe of my own body. I am but semi-conscious when there is a whisper of an invitation to turn over onto my back, a voice pulling me up from oblivion. I reluctantly reacquaint myself with the possibility of motion, direct my muscles and bones to rearrange themselves. I ease around by infinite degrees, eons passing before my back and buttocks carry the weight of me and I can submerge again, wordless.

I lie in time/space out-of-life. I lie in the totality of my life. My body is the microcosm and speaks all I need to know. Supine, the chronic pain in my lower back is amplified. I breathe even more deeply. The pain increases. I hear my mind instruct me to relax, breathe through the pain, make sounds. For the rest of the long massage I moan loudly with every exhale, and the moaning is for all of me, for all the losses, all the grief, for all the pain I know, have known. I want to moan it all away, to breathe release into my back, my life. Release does not come, and at the end I slowly turn on my side, pull my knees to my chest, weeping: "I am so tired of hurting, I am so tired of hurting."

Several mornings after the birthing Bethroot gestured, near the end of Silence, that neither Sami Slate nor her baby were in the cave. Just to make sure, I took the saucer of cat food Bethroot had in her hand and made my way to the stump, expecting to find Sami hidden in some far corner. But indeed she was not there. I hoped this was simply a sign that Sami must have moved her baby to a new spot. I wondered what had been the provocation, what scene had been enacted during the night. Silent time ended as I returned to the house to make waffles for a late breakfast for Bethroot and myself, trying to push aside the seed of worry planted in me. As we stood talking by the stove, I saw Sami through the northwest window, coming down the bank near the trailer. Bethroot went to feed her. The first waffle done, I removed the iron from the burner and went up to greet Sami Slate. She ate surprisingly little, went to do her toilet in the bushes, then sat somewhat listlessly in the sun and let us pet her. I so wanted to know where her baby was, so after a while I started up the path, hoping Sami would come close behind and lead me to her new nursery.

Sami walked a deer path into the forest but did not seem to be headed for a known destination. She meowed loudly and peered in all directions. This was strange behavior, quite different from what she'd been like the previous days, when she was silent as she approached her nest. Now she walked around as though not knowing where to go, and called out and listened, called out and listened. Bethroot came up the path and stood and watched the scene. "I think this might be a wild kitten chase," she offered. "I don't think Sami is going to show us where her kitten is right now.''

But as I watched Sami a lead weight landed on my chest: the kitten must be gone. I had been so intimate with Sami through this saga that I knew she would not be making such a clamor in the forest if in fact her kitten were tucked safely in some known place. The weight of yet another disappointment pulled me crying to the ground, as Sami walked around mewing for her baby. When she went over to the empty cave, I got up and followed her. She crept inside and called and came back out, still searching. Bethroot joined us as we trudged around in the forest, looking in other hollow stumps, the three of us in various states of shock. When I sank again to the forest floor, Sami came to my lap and nuzzled me, purred as I bent my head to hers. Between sobs I struggled to tell her I guessed some animal of the forest had taken her baby for nourishment, just as she had done so many times. How many mama mice had lost their little ones to Sami's hunger? How many times had she left bird feathers and squirrel tails on my bedroom floor after a meal she snatched from the forest? I cried, with no anger or judgment at the assumed predator, but from my own despair, and the pathos of this mother cat who called for her infant.

Sami stayed mewing in the forest when Bethroot and I decided we had better have our meal. She did not appear the rest of the day. I went looking for her in the evening but returned sadly after no sight or sound of her, and the next morning's search still brought no sign of Sami Slate. I resisted the thought that maybe she was gone now too, swallowed up by the forest as was her kit.

But Sami did eventually reappear, brought by hunger to her bowl, and over the next several days became more frequently visible, even slept on my lap one whole evening. I sensed there still remained a shred of watchfulness in her, an occasional alert listening for her kitten's call. As the weeks passed her body became sleek and trim again, her nipples shrank, milk sacs seemed to be dissolving. One night I carried her, purring, to my bed, but she was quickly off again, her Summer self too busy for a sedentary night.

I was not so buoyant as Sami became during those weeks, when the work of the land kept me busy and tired. I cut more firewood for the Winter, canned dozens and dozens of quarts of vegetables from the garden. I had intended to gather a great many bags of leaves for mulch, but the constant pain in my back, which had spread to my legs and feet, held me to twenty bags, and it took me three days to accomplish even that. Tormenting dreams of unfulfilled love left in their wake a growing doubt about my ability to ever bring easy and certain love to myself, except where the animals were concerned: in addition to the cats' sweet affection with me, wild birds chirped around me in the garden, and the deer were not currently eating my egg-sprayed flowers, so I spoke welcome to the does when they ambled near the house, their big trusting eyes matching my friendliness. Lady's aging arthritic body did not keep her from valiantly following me around as I worked, and she reminded me often of her unfailing availability for affection. Mailava, the family clown, tugged at both Lady and me to play; her antics made Lady move, and goaded me to laugh.

One day when I was using the trailer kitchen to can yet another batch of green beans, Sami came for loving, and for food. She was very hungry, though had breakfasted as usual earlier, ate yet another half a can, then wanted my lap, purred and nuzzled. I checked her one nipple which had remained pink and slightly swollen. I had been concerned there might be some infection, but now was astounded to discover that some hairs around the nipple were matted, as though someone had been sucking! Did Sami yet have her kitten secreted away in the forest?! But several days later the little glint of hope I had allowed myself was dulled when I found the sac beneath the nipple extremely hard and lumpy, the hair dry and free of tangle. She stayed around the house most of that day, and, for the first night in nearly three weeks, came with me to bed, curled in the bend of my arm and slept, leaving sometime during the night. The next morning she appeared from under the house after I had fed the hens. I checked her belly, concerned about what to do for the congestion that I worried must be painful, and, *voila!*, the gland was much smaller and soft, the fur around the nipple quite matted! The glint rekindled, blazed into a fire of gratitude, and I felt despair shifting to make room for joy again.

I sit on the barrel stool at the big window, lean my elbow on the wide sill. Below me is the garden, lush with Summer's abundance, the distant ridges softened by the dim late evening sun. Music from the tape player fills the house. The voice, the music are intimately familiar to me: I have listened to these songs, this woman singing, countless times – in rehearsal rooms, on performance stages, in our home, in my bed, in her arms.

I sit alone, look out the window at the land she, too, loved and remember . . . and remember . . . , her voice now ghost-like after these years of silence between us. The music continues with changing moods and variety of instrumental sound, from ballad to rock to a Latin beat. Her resonant voice joins the composer's lead and I open to the deepest truth of the loving still inside me. Suddenly the cave of my chest heaves with a moaning sob – all the sorrow, all the grief erupts in and through me. Her name rides on my wailing and she answers from the tape: "I hold myself when no one else will." Her voice is strong, bold, powerful, beautiful. "No Hay Razon . . .": there is no reason to live without heart.

The boiling sobbing washes me clear. I am pulled to the center of the house, the inner circle, to dancing. I push past the wanting for a woman to dance with, for. I push past the wanting for a lover, and dance for myself, for the joy, the pleasure of dancing. Shirtless and sun-browned, I dance alone, love the liquid voluptuous strength of my own body. My supple limbs pulse with the rhythm; my muscles, bones, breasts resonate with the sensuous vibration of the music. Darkness surrounds the circle as I dance by the candlelight from the round altar. I am a goddess, secreted in an ancient den. My dance is strong, bold, powerful . . . beautiful.

The mystery of Sami's offspring became more and more intense, intolerable in fact. Finally, one morning, I pleaded with her to take me to her kitten and the two of us set out for a walk. Missy Moonshine would often be found at the old barn down the hill so I thought to look there first. Sami followed close by as I walked slowly and kept gently encouraging her to guide me to her baby. We prowled around the barn together, Sami and I each poking our heads in likely places. No kitten. Then we ambled back up the path to the house and into the forest behind the rows of stacked firewood. Sami kept up a chatter, scouted, listened and watched, as we crept our way among the trees and brush on the slope, investigating around each rotting log, each mound of forest debris. She searched with me the whole way to where the old pit privy stood by the edge of the woods, but took me to no baby. I began to think this excursion, although pleasurable, might be fruitless, so chose the easier path again, headed back toward the house. Sami stopped to eat some grass, apparently losing interest in our task. I waited patiently, still determined to follow her to where surely there must be someone who sucked her breast. She paused in her eating, looked up the path, listened, saw neither of the dogs, nor Lillith, then turned to climb the steep bank on the opposite side of the path from where we'd just been hiking. I followed, awkwardly climbing over decaying roots and crumbling clay. At the top of the bank was a hollow stump Sami seemed to know. Inside, a small tunnel extended at a slight angle down into the earth farther than I could see. Sami stood at the entrance and purred. I reached down into the cave as far as my arm would go, but felt and heard nothing. Sami was the first to leave. Puzzled, but encouraged, I temporarily gave up the search and got started on the day's work.

Late in the afternoon, taking precaution that no one followed me, I returned to that hollow stump. I figured if I found Sami there, then certainly she must have her baby hidden inside. I approached as quietly as the climb permitted. Just as my face reached level with the stump, Sami suddenly appeared, the crumbling brown walls framing her sleek black fur. She purred as I petted her and gently rolled her over, to expose her wet and soft breast. I limited my exploding delight to quiet grins, honoring Sami's secret.

I went to the new cave frequently during the next few days until finally, four weeks after the disappearance, I saw two small black kitten feet sticking out behind a purring Sami. The mother moved aside so the kitten saw me too, reacted with a hiss, then scrambled down the tunnel to her safety. The next day she was there again when I arrived, and again hissed and speedily descended, so I petted and nuzzled her contented mother. Soon the tot reappeared and listened to me sing to her. I softly sang my love for her mother, her mother's love for me, stroking Sami all the while. The kitten watched and listened and did not withdraw when I slowly brought my hand to her, touched the top of her head with one outstretched fingertip. I cooed and courted her, with my hand, my voice, with my love for Sami Slate. After a while I showed her I had two hands, but this was one too many for her and she hissed her disapproval. I stayed there with the two of them an hour or so, watching the kitten, a small duplicate of Sami, play with the walls of the stump and her mother's long tail.

The next day I strolled happily down the path, anticipating the climb up the bank, and discovered it would not be required: both cats were lying in the grass a few feet to the side of the path below the stump. The kitten was no longer afraid of me, followed her mother's ease in taking and giving affection. Our lolling in the grass ended when Sami ordered us to her daughter's first walk. Sami led the way and I brought up the rear, following close by, but keeping an obedient demeanor, and walking at the kitten's pace. We stopped to relax next to the delphinium bed in front of the trailer, where Sami lay beside me and the baby climbed onto my lap for a few minutes' rest. Then kitten went to mama for a reviving snack, and we started out again. Sami turned into the forest and the little one had to work hard to get through the lowest-growing brush on the forest floor. A smiling Bethroot found us when we had our second rest stop and the kit allowed her to pick her up and rub her ears. As the walk continued, I began to understand Sami's intention: she was taking us on a protected route toward the woodstacks. Once there, she instructed the baby to enter a cave among the firewood logs, formed where two walls met at a diagonal. The little black body disappeared and stayed out of sight as Sami went to the trailer porch for breakfast. She came out much later, at Sami's beckoning, and sucked her fill. I packed my lunch and took my knitting and camera, and stayed there with them all the long day, watching the serene mother tend her young, who played and sucked and slept and played and sucked and slept.

*   *   *

It is dawn. Sami Slate thumps noisily up the steep staircase to my bedroom, stirs both me and the three month old kitten who has been sleeping between my arm and breast. I dreamily turn over to investigate the loud mewing and see that Sami brings a breakfast to her daughter, who bolts to the floor. A rabbit lies dead on the rug. It is a large animal for Sami to catch and kill and carry up the stairs. I watch as the two cats take turns eating. The mother gnaws off the rabbit's head, makes small pieces available for the catling. They eat into the steaming chest cavity until Sami has pushed the fur back as far as she can, then they leave their meal and slumber together on my bed.

The morning light is grey on the grey inert body on the floor. I sit beside it, imagine Sami in the forest, stalking, pouncing, killing. I sit beside the body of this rabbit and wonder if there are babies in the forest hungry for her breast. I caress the fur, stroke the soft belly, ask her spirit to help me understand these cyclic mysteries of birth and death, grieving and acceptance. I place myself in time an hour earlier, enfold this wild creature with my love as she becomes prey to my companion. I place myself in my future and look back at these years when I was easy prey for grief, when release bore the possibility of change. I enfold myself with faith in the healing promise of time.

I pull the rabbit's skin easily from her muscles, down over her back and legs, to expose the flesh. The cats' appetites are quickened and they return to their feasting. Soon Sami claims the body for her own, chews and cracks bones to swallowing size, pulls flesh and tendons to her hunger. I sit and watch the carcass disappear into Sami's body, the magical transformation of rabbit into cat. Cave Kidden plays happily with a leftover tuft of fur.

Barometric

This early morning I squatted to pee beside the woodshed – my first trip outside, made as soon as I dressed and went downstairs. The sky was blue, sparsely dappled with white, the colors of the day cheerful. As I squatted I smelled rain in the air. I had to smile at myself: the sky did not signal rain. There were no grey clouds hovering, no heavy wet messengers of an approaching storm. But my nose smelled rain coming, a precursory odor that touched my nostrils and some sense of knowing in me which lay deeper than my eyes' report. Some home-grown epistemology I knew to trust. I have lived here long enough, mixed my bloods (before menopause stopped those cycles), and sweat, and pee, and poop (composted) with this soil long enough, been cradled by this fold of the Mother's lap long enough to have learned a few things. While I peed my water on the Earth this morning, I knew before the day was out my urine would be washed by rain.

Sure enough, by late morning the sky had darkened, the day greyed, and a light rain came to kiss away the long dry Summer at last. Rain fell in a gentle staccato on the roof all afternoon as I knitted and mended, the house warmed by the woodstove. In the mere passing of a morning the seasons changed: just a few days ago a tired visitor lay naked in the hot sun beside the spent and dried cornstalks in the garden, while others of us sweated as we spread tarploads of leaves for mulch among the young plants in the Winter garden beds. Our work testified to our belief in Winter, belief in change, our faith the rains would come, would surely come soon, despite the sun's continued brightness. Two days passed, and I smelled the promise of rain as I squatted near the full woodshed.

The weather falls and brings with it the golden leaves of the lilacs and dogwoods; the clouds release the long-awaited draft that will revive the grasses gone brown on the knoll. Yesterday's dusty paths become heavy slick clay. The wetness darkens the greens of the firs and cedars, polishes the bronze bark of the sinewy madrones, and urges a cautious step on the now-slippery deck. The rain changes the seasons of the land, the body of the goddess, and the rain steals into my body and brings on the jointy ache of Autumn. I will not squat easily when I smell the harbinger of snow.

Making Family

The heavy frosts have come early this year and the wooly caterpillars look especially fat. Muphin's long, fluffy coat feels thicker than ever, and the deciduous trees have shorn themselves of any leafy excess which would add to a snowy Winter's weight. I wonder if we'll have a Winter like we had in '88, the year Muphin came to me as a youthful pup, the Winter we had more snow than we had ever had before. Not an easy Winter, not an always happy one. But an important one for me to remember.

Snow had begun falling during a late December night that year. When I awoke the next morning, I was delighted by the simple change of weather, cheered by the snow scenes out my bedroom windows. The layer of white was at least four inches thick on the ground, heavy on the trees, bending down many of the smaller ones near the path to the outhouse. When I passed them I wrapped my gloved hand around their trunks and shook them vigorously, releasing them from their snowburden. Most of them gladly rose from their weary bowing, but a few were permanently bent.

The snow changed what I had grown used to seeing, and thus *not* seeing, into a magical presence of white webs of leafless maple branches, corridors of fir leaning toward each other to make a canopy over the paths, and a pristine aura of cleanliness over all. The heavy snow released me from the heaviness of responsibilities, the weariness from all the work of maintaining this home. The snow slowed my normal pace as I trudged in my big warm boots through the nightsky's resistant gift. I was pulled to look around me, to even stop and just gaze wide-eyed at a trick of nature worked on a tree bough, or a yet-standing rose campion stalk.

Something about a snow swells the love in me and lets it come skipping out toward everything inviting my attention. Muphin had been the first I snowed my love on that morning, as she lay her fifteen pounds on my chest for a vigorous belly rub. "You are the best," I told her, kissing her with a loud smack on her tousled head, caressing her long floppy Lhasa Apso-Terrier ears. In the seven months since she had come to be with me, her constant love and silly antics kept my heart turned to joy, no matter what other, unwelcome, feelings may have come calling. I was so grateful for the miracle of her, felt extravagantly rewarded for all my care of Ladydog as she aged and finally died late in the prior Winter, for my waiting until I had recovered from the physical and emotional exhaustion of that tending before I brought this new companion to my life.

Muphin was fascinated with the snow, raced playfully around me when I went to feed the hens. She plowed muzzle-first into the drifts, searching out the odors beneath the powdery blanket. The snow balled up into big hard marbles on her long chest hair and short legs. She seemed glad for me to remove as much of the balls as I could, then she finished the job by standing beside the woodstove and licking them away as they melted.

The snowing continued for five days and, because it had become even colder, it was accumulating more, melting less during the day. The trees were spectacular: every twig and branch bore a thick white cloak, each tree standing in ermined majesty. I began to sense the power in the snow as well: the weight of it had the potential to snap large branches, even pull down trees, collapse roofs. The drifts made paths invisible and walking a major physical feat. With at least a foot of snow on our steep road, Bethroot and I knew neither her station wagon nor my compact pickup would make it up some parts of the hill. So, except for our big old farm truck's indomitable capacity to push past most anything in an emergency, we were snowed in. But I sure didn't mind this at all. I had a wanting to withdraw, to disappear into quiet peaceful solitude, at least as much as I could get of that, what with Bethroot, Mailava – who had become Bethroot's dog – Muphin, the four cats, and I all cramped together in the house.

A few days later the soft pattering on the lower roof was no longer snow falling – it was the snow melting just a bit from the cupola, encouraged by a light rain. Bethroot and I and the dogs took a short walk down toward the east side, as far as the little spring, marvelling in the snow scene. The snow was as deep as Muphin was tall, so she soon asked to be carried when she had enough of bunny-hopping her way along the path. As we walked, Bethroot and I talked about the workshop we had agreed to present at the *Lesbian Family* Conference in Portland later in the Winter. We knew we wanted to inspire other Lesbians with our story, be an example of transforming from a troubled lovership to an almost harmonious land partnership, and we wanted to give women a taste of the magic we create here, the goddess-love guiding us through the seasons of the land, the seasons of our lives. We each had begun to search through our journals looking for material to share about the twelve years of partnering we had thus far been doing. Alas, we were finding so much of the sorrow and pain those years had held. We asked ourselves, and each other, what of our experience we wanted to share, what was important. Dared we be so vulnerable as to include our propensity for disagreement over almost anything, the pain we caused each other, past and current, the enmity between us that sometimes blotted out all caring? Could we present ourselves truthfully without speaking of all that?

We each continued to puzzle with this in the following weeks, slowly weaving a tapestry to show us in our many guises. I was particularly aided in this process by a lesson inadvertently learned with Muphin one beautiful February day. I remember the sun was so bright and warm in a sometimes clear blue, sometimes billowy white-clouded, sky. I thought surely Muphin and I must go out for a walk in such fair weather; I needed to give myself some fresh air and exercise, and a break from the tedium of hand-copying excerpts from my journals for the upcoming workshop, to flesh out the basic script Bethroot was writing. She had gone to town for the day, so, except for me, the land was peopleless and quiet. Muphin and I set out for the barn first. It had been months since I'd walked down in that direction, and I wanted to see what state the half-century-old barn was in after all the heavy snow, which by then was melting quickly from the house roof. I discovered the barn continued to look much like it had for years: the roof rafters barely hanging on in some places, shingles missing here and there. The hand-hewn boards of the siding retained the orange-brown beauty of their natural aging, accented by the Winter wet.

I did not stay down there long. Although Muphin was reluctant to backtrack so soon, I had noticed a few of the hens strolling nearby, and I wanted her out of their way, not yet sure I could trust her behavior with them. But at least we were walking and she got excited as we headed up the path, which I needed to climb slowly in my heavy coat and boots. Suddenly she took off, and paid no attention at all to my command to come back. Soon I heard hens squawking. I ran up the steep hill as best I could, yelling on the way "No! Muphin, Muphin, no!!" But she was beyond any attempt to control her, within seconds had a chicken chased all the way back down to the top of the orchard. I was after them as fast as I could go down the brushy hillside, could soon make out that Muphin had grabbed the hen in her mouth and was shaking her as the hen screamed. With my rage full-blown I yelled at Muphin my loudest "NO!!" Something must have snapped in her then, because she dropped the hen, looked up at me and backed off from her prey as I ran toward her. The hen lay in the snow, her beak opening and closing as her breast heaved, alive but silent. Muphin distanced herself further and watched as I picked up the hen and held her to my chest. There were lots of feathers on the snow, red-gold against the white. I quickly searched for any injury and was horrified to discover a large patch of skin had been torn from the bird's back, exposing fat and muscle, the wound oozing a little blood and cloudy fluid. I don't know which felt worse: my grief at the hen's suffering, or my horror at Muphin for what she had done. I stood there a minute or so to catch my breath, comforting the hen, staring in shock at Muphin. I stepped angrily toward her. She backed away. But she was right behind me when I got to the bottom garden gate, so I grabbed her with one hand, smacked her nose sharply with my fingers, and firmly pushed her away from me and the hen with a scolding: "Bad dog!"

We came up through the garden to the house where I quickly set about to care for the hen. I doused the large wound with some home-made Hypericum oil, and forced some down her throat as well. She stayed quiet through this treatment, either grateful for the rescue and my care, or too traumatized to protest. I put some rags into a cardboard box near the back door and placed the chicken inside, just room enough for her to lie comfortably, with a sense of enclosure and safety. A screen weighted down with a couple hammers made a secure cover, and a cloth over that provided dark seclusion. I figured it would not be good for her to be with the other hens, and she needed more warmth than the drafty hen-house could provide on a Winter night.

I think I must have been in some shock myself because, although I was exhausted, I went back outside to repair the swinging dog door in the fence up by the main gate. One of its rope hinges had broken some time before, and the door hung askew, so, although Muphin had never used it, it was possible for her to get out if she wandered near there and saw a hen on the lane, and the wild instinct to chase and kill overcame her again. I'd been meaning to fix the door, but hadn't gotten around to it, thinking the hens weren't venturing out into the snow much as yet, and I guess hoping Muphin could be trusted to do them no harm. She was sitting beside the woodbin as I went out the door; my "Stay!" was angry. She knew my mood, did not follow me – probably the first time since we'd been together that I had left the house without her. I fixed the door quickly and returned to the house, giving up my original intention for a longer walk, fearful of leaving the hen untended. I didn't think either the dogs or cats would be able to remove the screen, but I did not want to risk any further ugly scenes, and I wanted to assure the hen of a quiet rest. I disturbed her only a little when I sprinkled goldenseal powder into and all around the big oozing hole in her back.

Muphin had gone into the living room, but then came closer when I sat crying with anger and sadness on a stool near the workbench, on which I had relocated the hen's box. My tears grew to a dragging misery at feeling so estranged from Muphin. I appealed to her through my sobbing: "Oh, Muphin, it feels rotten to be this angry at you. Without you as my trusted friend I'm so lonely." More crying. She watched and listened, unmoving. I sternly lectured her that she cannot be in this family and be a wild dog too; that with this love, this security, this home, there come responsibilities. She had to learn there are restrictions on her freedom, some fetters in this life. There are shoulds and shouldn'ts in the way we live here, and respect must be given to all of us. "You are not allowed to harm another creature in this family," I repeated again and again, while her big brown eyes locked with mine.

I went into the inner circle of the house then, sat on my meditation pillow before the altar and cried some more. Muphin came and lay beside me in her usual place, snuggled her head against my knee. No doubt she trusted I would not further punish her there: when I sit on this pillow I become my calmest, and perhaps wisest, self. Eventually my tears were replaced by deep breathing and I could empty myself of the anger, settle into the exhaustion of my body, and play back to myself the harsh lecture I had given to Muphin. As I listened to my words I realized what I had said to her applies to all of us, Bethroot and myself included. "With this love and this security, this home, there come responsibilities," I had instructed Muphin. And surely that same code applied to us two Lesbians who do reap love and lots of security by sharing this home. Yes, there was often enmity between us, but we were also growing more accepting of each other, and each bore a gratitude for the other's companionship in the keeping of this temple, the working of this land. Longevity alone gave evidence of our bonding, the depth and sureness of our commitment. We were indeed creating family, making it up out of our real experience with each other. And this included anger and resentments, impatience and frustration many, too many, days. We were each bonded to this land and to the vision we had created and nurtured together of *Fly Away Home*. Clearly we had to go to the conference with the intention to share the unhappy side of this family too, because that was a part of our truth, a part that pushed each of us to constantly renew, and thus deepen and enliven, our choice to continue to create the beauty we enjoyed.

I cared for the hen diligently, made a four-foot square pen for her, with a screen on top and covered with cloths. I placed food and water and one of the nesting boxes from the henhouse inside, and soon she was eating and drinking, and standing or sitting on top of the box. The goldenseal had caked a solid crust over the big hole so there was no further bleeding or loss of other fluid, and no evidence of infection. When I saw her stand and fluff out her wings I knew the danger had passed, so within a week from the awful event she was back with the flock. Muphin and I mended too, our playful loving returned, our bonding deepened through adversity.

I wish I could say that Muphin never again bothered the hens, and that Bethroot and I have lived happily ever after, like the fairy tales go. But there were more chases and injuries until Muphin finally understood what adaptation of her temperament was required of her, and there have been some awful scenes between Bethroot and me since that workshop where we bravely told our multiple truths. We still have much to learn about making friendship, much to invent about making family, as the seasons and dramas of our lives educate us gradually closer to mutual respect and acceptance.

Recycling

It had been about nine years since Izetta hung her grandmother's old tin Revere lantern from my bedroom ceiling. The countless little slits, struck in a delicate pattern in the thin rusty brown metal, projected a candle's light into flame-yellow dots all around the circular room. After Izetta moved back to the city I was glad her family heirloom still hung in my home, testament to the depth we had shared, to the bond that might survive our separation.

Izetta was long gone by the time I built the Poogoda, the state-of-the-art two-seater composting outhouse which replaced the old rank pit privy. I moved the lantern there, where it could add its rustic beauty to the primitive elegance of my architectural style. Then two years later I added a big four-unit poop-composting bin. With all the visitors Bethroot and I had, especially around our quarterly gatherings at the Solstices and Equinoxes, and Hallowmas, plus participants in the Summer workshops we were still teaching back then, the 33-gallon plastic garbage cans we had been using for collection, composting, and storage turned out to be inade-quate. Not only were the four cans too few for the accumulation, the anaerobic process they created produced a sludge and slurry end-product which I was not eager to work with. I did laboriously mix some of the oldest can's well-composted contents with peat moss, and used it in new plantings in my flower garden. The pleasing odor of the mix was reminiscent of rich barnyard, like the floor of Jennie and Gaelyn's goat barn, well over a foot thick with hay and manure. It was very satisfying, a work of magic, to place my own, and countless others', droppings around the hosta, cyclamen, clematis . . . to return to the Earth, transformed, what she had given to us from the vegetable garden.

At about that time I started recycling my pee as well. Mixed with five parts water, sprinkled on the area around the house, the golden liquid worked a minor miracle on the once-bald clayey earth, raising a green grass carpet with its plentiful nitrogen. I could see the difference almost daily, and felt such keen gratitude for this partnership with the Earth, my body and hers giving nourishment and pleasure back and forth.

Grass grew and flowers bloomed, fed by our own decay, flowers I had only dreamed of when Izetta's mother, June, came here to visit for her 64th birthday, during Izetta's first Winter on the land. June stayed in my bedroom where her mother's lantern yet hung. She was delighted to see it, remembered an old family story of it hanging in a barn when her mother, the first Izetta, was a child. I wondered if a great-grandmother had ever lit a candle in it and watched the light sparkle from the tiny slits. I remember that visit well, remember massaging June's feet as we sat by the woodstove, while Izetta and her mother talked about the past, about Izetta Jewel, the grandmother for whom both of these women were named, Izetta the second becoming June, short for "junior." At that time, I had not seen my own mother for fifteen years, so I studied June closely, her age the same as Rita's, born just four days apart. I massaged a mother's feet, while she and Izetta talked quietly and shared their grief about the death the year before of Izetta Jewel, the "grand mere."

Nine years later, while I worked on the composting bin, June, just 73, was dying of breast cancer. Working alone each day in the silent forest, I had plenty of time to think about Izetta, about her having recently taken a new lover, about her keeping vigil with her rapidly weakening mother, about living and dying, decaying and recycling. I constructed the walls of the bin from boards salvaged when the old privy was dismantled; scraps left over from various other projects became the plywood partitions. The corner posts were taken up from the vineyard: though they had rotted at the soil line, their tops were still useful. The roofing paper for the lids dated from excess left thirteen years before by the former owners of this land. And all of it painted against the weather with used crankcase oil saved over the years. A project built on the gleanings from elsewhere, to waste nothing, to know the value – the gift – of endings, of what is finished, of change.

One day late in April I worked especially late on the bin. It was nearly seven o'clock when I put my tools away, covered the lumber with a tarp, and carried the sawhorses to the nearby Poogoda, where the side-roof would protect them from the unpredictable Oregon Spring weather. As I neared the shelter, some motion caught my eye: the tin lantern was swinging on its wire, making a wide and vigorous arc. I put the sawhorses away, then stood and watched as the lantern swung with an energy not mirrored by any tree about, not even a leaf or spider's thread. I propped myself against a tree, joined the twilight stillness of the wider scene and focused on the unceasing swing of the lantern. Minutes passed, and more . . . and more . . . and still the lantern moved in its quarter circle, as though some hand playfully pushed it. A grandmother's hand, perhaps? or a great-grandmother's? I watched in delight, and easy belief, felt visited by a motherline of Izettas.

Darkness, and hunger, pulled me from the lantern and the day's work. In the following weeks I finished the construction, and the hundred or so gallons of stored sludge were layered with grass mowed from the new lawn, buckets of kitchen scraps, and leaves raked from beneath the madrones, filling two of the bins. By late Spring the new system for recycling our womanure was well underway, and June had died. When I applied the rich fluffy compost to the new flower beds the following year, I added some to the boxes at the Poogoda as well, where gay pink and red primroses bloomed beneath the old lantern.

Skunk in the Henhouse

February began with a thin and tentative covering of snow. Bethroot had gone off for a week to visit her friends up north, and I was grateful for the respite of a week alone on the land and in the house the two of us still shared. I had a lot of troubled thinking to do, some things to puzzle through about my life, my home, about the patterns between Bethroot and me that were stealing the sense of peace we each deserved. The dogs, big Mailava and little Muphin, and the four cats were perfect company as I settled in to fill the days with all-too-rare solitude.

My first night alone I was awakened at 1:30 a.m. by a loud banging around in the henhouse, and a hen screaming. Since the henhouse is located just a few feet out my backdoor, the sounds were frighteningly audible. A hen being attacked can scream an alarm to pierce even the deepest sleep. I rushed out of bed still groggy, and began to pull on some socks as the cry continued. I figured the cause was the Spotted Skunk who had, a few weeks earlier, killed Charity's Child, one of the older hens. My attempt to catch the intruder then with the Hav-a-Heart trap had failed: she had managed a Houdini-escape, leaving behind a stench in the henhouse which kept some. of our ten free-ranging chickens away for days. Four of them still had not given up roosting in the trees. I guessed they felt safer on limbs twelve to fourteen feet from the ground than huddled on the roost in the house, easy prey for a trespasser. The memory of that scent slowed my work with the socks, made me question just what I thought I could do in the middle of the night to a skunk attacking the hens. What effect could I possibly have? I'd probably only get skunked myself.

"I can't do it," I groaned aloud, and gave up the rush, resigned to losing yet another hen, whom I'd probably find dead first thing in the morning. Then I'd set out the trap again and hope for better luck than last time.

The crashing and squawking intensified, and I quickly did an about-face. Maybe I would not be able to stop the murder, but I could not just go back to bed and ignore the hen's pealing distress. I got on the socks and my bathrobe, and ran down the stairs to grab my boots, coat, hat, and a flashlight, and raced off outside and down the back porch stairway to the henhouse. I shined a spotlight through the framed poultry fencing door to reveal the small black and white furry creature who had the old Barred Rock pinned on the floor, yanking at her neck. I yelled at the skunk, got her attention, then grabbed the first tool at hand off the outer wall – a grass whip – opened the door and banged the handle on the floor, hoping the noise and my anger would at least frighten the skunk into letting go of the hen. It worked, and the skunk took refuge in one of the nesting boxes in the corner.

Sister Barred lay motionless on the bedding of dry leaves, the five other hens confused and astir on the nearby roost. I wondered why they had not come to the old hen's aid. Surely the six of them could have given that skunk quite a lesson, and enough incentive to get out of there and leave them alone. Why didn't these big birds with their strong thick beaks fight back? Their only instinct seemed to be flight, to run from danger instead of facing and subduing it.

So then I had the skunk cornered and five hens still easy prey, Sister Barred inert on the floor. Much to their dislike, I shoved each hen out the high chicken-size doorway to the outdoor ramp, pushed them to fly down to their enclosed yard. They squawked nervously as they disappeared into the darkness, 1:30 a.m. not a time they were accustomed to being out and about. While I was getting them all out, the Barred Rock suddenly jumped up and let out a screech bespeaking her vitality, though I think she was somewhat worse for the experience of being in death's mouth. I got her outside too, and closed the little door, sealing the prey out and the predator in.

We had gotten into the practice of leaving this door open all the time, so the hens could come and go as they pleased. For nearly fourteen years there had never been any problem with intruders, whom we theorized found the narrow ramp, and the doorway six feet from the ground, too exposed for stealthy hunting. Old theories, like habits, are hard to give up, and the recent and current predatory episodes did not sufficiently jar this one. Besides, I was loathe to cut off any possible escape the hens could have, especially if, as I assumed, the skunk was getting in some other way.

I fetched the Hav-a-Heart trap from under the house where I had stored it after that last attempt to catch this troublemaker. I did not have a better plan for this incident, nor was I thinking much past emergency, so I baited the trap with pieces of apple stuck with peanut butter onto the bait pan, and set it close to the nesting boxes. I called a blessing of safety to the hens in their night-time exile from their home, and crossed some mental fingers for the skunk to be unable to withstand the temptation of the bait.

Sleep did not come easily. I was all astir myself after the rescue mission that, thankfully, worked after all. However, I still had a skunk in the henhouse to deal with. *Skunk in the henhouse.* I brooded over the phrase. It aligned with my sense of there being something all wrong with this scene: not just in the henhouse, but in the home Bethroot and I had been sharing those fourteen years, a few of them in the collective of four, then just the two of us again for the last six. Our ways of relating to each other had not kept pace with the changes we each had made, and the house, which had seemed roomy enough when we first began to make a home of it, had been growing smaller in recent years. Though Bethroot had her bedroom in the cedar yurt up the hill, I felt a cramping happening between and around us. The skunk in the henhouse was like the malaise that had intruded upon our lives; I wondered what it would take to rid ourselves of it.

I did finally get to sleep, the morning well begun before I awoke. Soon I heard a metallic crash outside, and hoped this meant the skunk was in the trap. But no rush this time. I dressed at my normal pace, and greeted Mailava on my way out the back door. I could see the trap from the back porch and, sure enough, there was white and black fur inside.

I covered the trap with an old cloth to quiet its tenant and removed it far from the henhouse, so the hens could come around for their breakfast. Most refused to go into the house to the food hopper. I couldn't blame them: the pungent skunk scent must have smelled like danger to them.

Around noon I put the trapped skunk inside the canopy on the back of my old pickup and drove, with Muphin along, down the hill to the county road and on east a few miles to where the county maintenance stops, at the beginning of BLM country, where there is a turn-off leading to the creek. I placed the trap on the snow at the edge of the forest, removed the cloth, and opened the door. It took only a short moment for the skunk to realize freedom was a step away. Her fur looked regal against the white snow as she scrammed her way among the nude brush and into the woods. "No hard feelings," I called after her, then added a scold: "but don't come back up the mountain to my henhouse!"

The next day a fierce wind picked up and slammed down the metal roof on the garden compost bin, pushed and pulled on the trees as though to carry them off. I studied the force of the wind moving like a wave through the cedar lattice awning hanging over the deck, listened to it howl around the house as though to spin a cocoon to encase me in an inner silence. The wind was a welcome companion as I busied myself indoors with solitary Winter tasks: mended and knitted, cooked up a big pot of vegetable stew to last me a while, made cards with my photographs of last Summer's flowers, wrote in my journal. Sometimes I just stared out a window and watched the trees, whose limbs blustered around while their trunks stayed firmly rooted in the earth. For some months a part of me had been restless, discontent, reaching, but I homed this land as tenaciously as the trees, rooted in the certainty of my life here. In the prior few weeks I had been plagued with what I had misinterpreted as loneliness: it vanished in the sweet simplicity of aloneness.

The next two days were fairly uneventful; the wind ended her visit, a light snow fell, pulling me deeper into the silence and closed-in feeling the snowy weather created. I loved the solitude which carried no compromise, no daily adapting to someone else's temperament, no arguments about housekeeping chores, or sched-ules to balance. I luxuriated in being cut off from the world beyond my sight and hearing, with no one to remind me of my limitations: no one to call my attention to birdsong lying beyond my ears' reach, no one I had to ask to repeat speech so I could understand and respond. Instead, what I *could* see and hear expanded, filled up the universe without contradiction. I looked out the window to a scene that struck me with its beauty as though for the first time. "I live here! – on this land, in this house," I mused, leaning on the kitchen counter and gazing at the evergreen forests and snow-covered ridges.

On the fourth night I was asleep by 9:00, then suddenly came so fully awake at first I thought it must be morning, as though I had been a long night in bed and it was time to stretch to a new day. But it was too dark for all that. The beam of the flashlight on the clock showed it was not quite 4:00 a.m. Even an early-to-bed did not warrant being awake that early. Nevertheless, I lay wide awake, cozy and not discontent, wondering why I should be so alert. Maybe minutes passed, maybe longer, when the unmistakable odor of skunk hit my nostrils. "Oh no!" I thought, and hoped the scent was carried by one of the cats, or even Mailava, just back from a nocturnal foray into the forest. My mind clung to hope, my body so very reluctant to leave the warm comfort, and cuddly Muphin, for another nightmarish adventure. But presently the sounds of severely upset chickens signalled the intense scent had not come from downstairs, but through the half-opened window at my head, so I knew a critter was bothering the hens again. Now my "Oh, no!" was audible, as well as a moaning "Not again."

It did not take long to get on my hen-protecting costume, and get down to the henhouse. Sure enough, there was the Spotted Skunk, just diving for cover in a nesting box. Four of the seven hens who had roosted inside that night had already fled the scene, with the three remaining ones in various states of confusion and fear. The Barred Rock jolted up from a corner – she had apparently been easy prey again, the one unstable on her feet. I gently pushed the others out the little doorway, then picked up Sister Barred, carried her outside, and set her carefully on the ground. I got the trap and repeated the baiting procedure I'd done earlier in the week, though when I got back to the henhouse with it, the skunk was not to be seen. I checked the nesting boxes and all around inside the eight-by-ten-foot house, but no skunk. Did it climb the roost and sneak out the little door? Or was there a hole in the floor or wall, just big enough to let this quart-size critter through if it stretched itself thin enough? I inspected thoroughly and found a narrow crack in the siding, probably not adequate for a even a small skunk's passage, but I needed to take some further action, so went to the workbench in the house for a piece of plywood, hammer and nails, and a brighter flashlight. Returning to the henhouse, I felt the urge to look under it to see if the skunk was hiding there. Yep! The beam from my flashlight glared off a set of staring yellow eyes and shined on the black and white spotted coat. But wait!, there were two sets of those eyes! Two skunks!! Was there a message out in the neighborhood that I served good apples and peanut butter?

There I was, in the middle of the night, dressed in flannel pajamas and other layers, armed with a flashlight and one small Hav-a-Heart trap. There were two skunks looking at me mischievously from under the henhouse, eight hens in various states of vulnerability here and there in the yard and in the adjacent forest, and two still quietly roosted on a buttress under the roof extension, where they had begun the night. I felt rather overwhelmed by the task at hand. How to protect all the hens from two skunks at large, with one trap? I accepted my predicament and set out to do the best I could, placed the trap inside near the nesting boxes, hoping to lure at least one skunk back to the scene of the crime, and entrapment. Then I started carrying hens one-by-one to the forest, where I intended to place them in the trees and be fairly sure they'd be safe for the night. Unfortunately, they could not tell my good intentions from the skunk's murderous ones, so squawked in great protest as I carried them, stumbling my way through the snow-wet brush. And then they each went into their second line of self-protection: go limp. So when I attempted to place them on a limb, they'd just let themselves fall off. I got only one of them secured on a limb and watched two others flutter to the ground. This was exasperating, to say the least. Here I was trying to save their lives and they decided to play dead!

This seemed sheer stupidity to me. "What's the matter with you?" I yelled at them. "And why don't you fight back when a skunk is after you?" I was angry, and I was worried. I don't know which of those made my eyes tearful, but I gave up on the hens and trudged back through the brush to the henhouse and had another look underneath. Both skunks were still there, patiently waiting, I supposed, for this comic scene I was enacting to end, so they could get on with their marauding. Dammit, I wasn't done yet. Back again to the forest where those two passive birds still sat on the forest floor. I managed to get one of them up on the highest branch I could reach with bird and flashlight in hand, but the other, one of the smaller Buffies, became alert enough to know she did not want to be handled by the likes of me again. As I approached her, she walked steadily beyond my reach further into the forest. And that spelled the end of my heroic efforts.

I called out loud enough for all protagonists to hear: "There are skunks out here," to the hens, with a sigh. "Maybe one, maybe more of you could die yet tonight," I warned. Then, with a whimper, to the skunks, "Please leave the hens alone." The truth was I was not in control of this situation. I had no means, nor wanted them, to kill the skunks and thus end their pestering, nor could I prevent the hens from being attacked. I had to accept this scene had many players, and I was but one of them, and a rather ineffectual one at that.

I changed into clean dry pajamas and snuggled up with Muphin two hours after the beginning of this episode, delighted to find a spot beneath the covers she had kept warm. Of course I was wide awake with hens and skunks on my mind, fearful of hearing another round of squawking. I kept puzzling about those hens who had gone limp when I had tried to give them to the safety of a tree. What instinct told them to play dead in the face of the danger they were in? What kind of a ploy was that for a predator who wouldn't be put off by their passivity, which in fact made them easily attacked? And why didn't all of them gang up on their assailant who was, after all, smaller than most of them; why didn't they beat their wings, and strike with their claws, and peck as a ferocious group to defend themselves?

The forest stayed silent as I pondered all this, searching in the storehouse of what I knew, for possible understanding of what I did not know. It came to me that the natural predator of the chickens is not the Spotted Skunk at all, but rather the Hawk, a daytime hunter, who swoops from great heights to kill a moving prey. I have heard it said a chick knows the meaning of the shadow of a Hawk passing overhead, even before it hatches from the egg. And I have seen our flock run for cover when even vultures circle nearby in a bright sky. But perhaps when flight from the Hawk's swift attack seems impossible, the hen goes limp, plays dead to fool her winged predator who, unless nearly starving, has no taste for carrion. A smart scheme, I allowed, and my respect for my hens returned somewhat. Be that as it may, such a tactic seemed ill-used for the nocturnal skunk, whose interest is in a still, unmoving, sleeping bird in the first place.

All this brought my own role in this scene into focus. If left to their own pure instincts, my big birds would not be sleeping on an artificial roost in a little house, with the small open door high on the wall made for their convenience, but, as I began to suspect, available for intruders as well. They would be in the trees at night – as some of my hens did in fact prefer – where they would be fairly safe from the likes of skunks and other hunters of sleeping flesh. It was in *my* interest to want them in the coop, so they'd lay their eggs there, and go broody in the nesting boxes there, when I could give them store-bought chicks to raise. It was my greed for their produce and service that placed them at risk to predators their genes knew no defense against, except to run and squawk if they could, and then to lie still in hope of seeming repulsive.

This understanding made me into less than the hero I had fancied myself; it humbled me into letting go of my complaint about the hens' behavior. The silence continued, and sleep came at last.

The next morning all the hens were present and whole-of-body when I tossed the grain into their yard. The trap was still set in the house, the bait untouched. I did not close the gate to the yard for the morning as I usually do, to keep the hens close to the laying boxes for whatever eggs they might leave. I figured the fright they had had during the night might cancel any laying, and I did not want them to feel at all caged. When late afternoon's dusk came, I checked in on them and saw most of them had gone to roost in the trees, with the old Barred Rock in the henhouse accompanied by two others, all three huddled cozily together on the roost. I finally decided to close the little door, thus imprisoning the hens, gambling the doorway was the skunk's entry, but left the trap set just in case I was wrong.

And the morning thereafter, everything was as I had left it the night before. All the hens came quickly for their grain, and we went back to the usual routine of the morning's restriction to the yard. That night I set the trap under their house and continued to close the little door nightly.

The snow, which had been falling lightly for almost two weeks, now thickened, with several inches accumulating two days after I'd started closing the hens' door at night. The previous pattern of snow and melt, snow and melt, gave way to a thin blanket on the ground that would linger a while. I was content with the cold snowy weather, had plenty to do. I cut up an old denim skirt I had found in some other country dyke's freebox and made myself some aprons, one for the kitchen and one for my carpenter's work-bench. Every once in a while I took a break from the old treadle sewing machine to watch the Black-Capped Chickadees busy at the feeder just out the window, and stare at the slumbering garden and the snow-trimmed apple trees down in the orchard. I could make myself an apple pie from the stored harvest, and the pie would be wholly for myself. With the growing solitude had come a depth of security, comfort, and contentment. Alone, I expanded to fill up the space, and knew a sense of completion. I lacked for nothing.

The snow stayed on the ground, with more lightly falling, the 25° temperature making it fairly dry and fluffy. I heard nothing disturbing around the henhouse for a few days, then finally discovered the trap had an occupant when I routinely checked it one morning late in the week. I assumed she was not able to get into the henhouse so settled for the apple and peanut butter on the bait pan as secondary fare. I maneuvered the trap with its catch into a large paper bag and had a close-up view as the skunk aimed her spray out the side of the trap. Not a direct hit on me or my clothing, thank goodness, but close enough to make me respect the skunk for certainly being a creature with strong defenses.

That close-call with skunk spray gave me cause to think further about the hens' seemingly lackadaisical attitude. Perhaps the hens had yet more instincts I had not given them credit for, namely that fight is not always the best procedure. Perhaps their apparent passivity was in fact the best defense against a skunk who would surely spray them if attacked. I reasoned that if I were only a few inches taller than a skunk, the threat of that musk projected into my eyes, and likely covering my whole body, would be a convincing cause for retreat, for noncombat. Maybe avoiding conflict took as much skill and devotion to self-preservation as a fight, an idea that might well apply with good results to house-mates/land partners. Bethroot and I had gotten into an easy habit of disagreements over almost anything, which often built to angry shouting, leaving me depressed for days. I might take instruction from the hens, and realize many of those arguments were not worth having.

I dispatched the second skunk as I had the first, down at the creek. The temperature warmed slightly during the morning and the snow changed to a light on-and-off rain. I wanted to teach the hens that their house was safe for night-time perching, so kept them closed in their yard all day. I did not feel too bad about this restriction because they tended not to wander about much on a rainy day anyhow, preferring, like me, the comfort of their dry house. But by late in the afternoon, when it was time to roost, a Buffy and a Red were clucking nervously as they paced the fence line near their gate, no doubt wanting the trees. Two others were perched on the buttress under the eave. Those two I plucked from their vulnerable roost and lifted them past the small door which I pulled shut enough so they'd stay inside. Then I turned my attention to the other two on the ground, not knowing how I was going to persuade them to go inside. I heard a clucking coming not from either of them, but sounding above my head, from the cedar that serves as a corner post in the fence, and, by darn, if Biggest Buffy wasn't up there on a limb. She would have had to fly fairly vertically to reach the lowest limb, a six foot jump, an impressive accomplishment for a heavy chicken. And she was not satisfied yet, kept fidgeting and clucking as though she needed something better. I did not feel very happy about her spot in the cedar either, because she could easily turn about and land outside the hens' yard, but inside the fence which protects my flower beds from her scratching. She was maybe solving one problem, but creating another one for me.

Clearly, I was not going to have all the hens in the house for that night, so I opened the gate. The two on the ground rushed out and into the forest, headed for their perch of choice I assumed. I nudged Biggest Buffy off the cedar branch and she went flying with a cackle to join her "wild" sisters. I fastened the little door from inside the house, bid the seven semi-willing sleepers goodnight, and placed fresh bait in the trap under the house.

I slept the sleep of angels that night, deep and undisturbed, and had another skunk in the trap the next morning. Unable to tell if this was yet a different member of the team or a rerun of what was getting to be an old movie, I figured I'd better take this one further away, far enough so there would be no chance of a reappearance. The day was sunny and warm, a nice day for a drive, so I decided I'd take the caged skunk the fifteen miles west to town, then on out Dole Road to where I could get down to a beachy area of the South Umpqua River. There I could release it to a welcoming setting.

After a filling breakfast, I stowed the skunk in the back of the pickup as before, then noticed the gas gauge warned me to stop in town for a fill-up. When I got there I guess the truck announced itself rather dramatically, because the station attendants began laughing and talking about "polecat perfume." The man who washed my windows jawed on and on about the skunks he'd shot, and the ones he had run over, which he seemingly assumed was what had happened to me. I was not about to inform him otherwise, though it might have been fun to see what would have happened if I had explained: "Oh, no I have a live one in a covered trap in the back of the pickup, and she's probably spraying right now!"

A few miles north of town I turned off onto a dirt track which led to where the river, swollen now with rain and snow-melt, licked the brushy banks. The skunk made her dash for the shadows in the brush, and Muphin and I started back home. This would be my last day alone, and I looked forward to savoring the hours left in my singularity, to a meal I'd make to please myself, to a lingering hot bath that would wash away the remaining suggestion of skunk scent. As I drove the winding route, passing green cover-cropped fields and nibbled-down pastures, patches of evergreens, a barren orchard whose trees might feel a pruner's hand before the month was out, I imagined a future that had more possibilities, with neither flight nor fight, but rather solitude as the way of my life.

Photo by Judith Moore

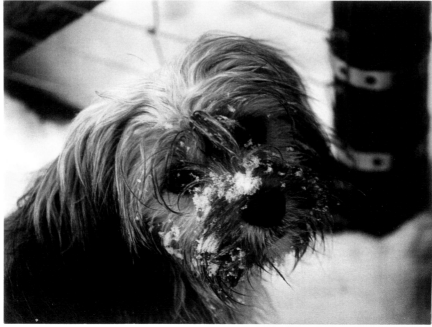

Photo by Robin Earth

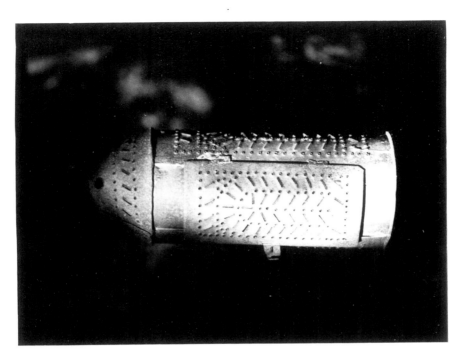

The Hills Are Alive

On what would have been the tenth anniversary of our ring ceremony, I dream of my former mate, and all the old passion and aching are stirred up. I dream her open and smiling, loving and warm, but she stays just beyond my reach; she is flirtatious and teasing, intimate but untouchable. This scene is too hard for me; I must get away from her, though flight gives no relief. I awake crying, for the lack of love, for having to withdraw mine.

It had been ten years that early Spring since we exchanged the rings we had made to honor our loving, and six years since we parted in anguished drama. Six years, and I could still dream of her with longing, still awaken with the image of her as real as the dawning sun painting the tops of the trees below the garden, as real as an evening wind racing through my hilltop forest, the trees flailing their limbs about, swaying mightily as though to follow the wind's direction. Part of me was blowing around, restless, reaching, buffeted, but I stayed barnacled to grief. This state was not how I imagined myself for my fifties. I expected to be peacefully settled in a loving and secure relationship, going about my life with a sense of completion and fulfillment. Failing that, I expected to be at least wise enough to create satisfaction with my lot in life.

But the dreams continued: I am with her and her new partner, the woman she now calls her mate; we have all sat down to a meal together. I watch their easy loving. My insides begin to howl. I am hungry, so very hungry, for what they have.

I was stuck. I wanted to be done with this pain, be released from its hold on me, its invasion of too many of my nights, and some of my days. It was absurd to be such ready prey for despair when I lived in the midst of such abundance: of trees and flowers, food grown with my own labor, the great bowl of sky and miles of ridges; there was strengthening work to do; there was blessed silence. There was all the love I could wish for in Muphin's always-available soft brown eyes, wagging tail, cuddly little fluffy body. Because I used to share this home with my mate, I could be pulled from the happy knowing of its bounty to a depressing sense of what was missing.

I needed to break through this despondency, take myself beyond the past and forge contentment within myself. I needed to go to where there was a measure of unfamiliarity, where the past could not whisper from the corners, or shadow the face of my own shining. I wanted to be spirit-fed.

My emerging vision was modest. I did not need, nor could I afford, a long-distance adventure. My sights were not on a foreign country or great physical challenge. I wanted simple Earth, openness, height, sky, beauty, peace – like home, but with a few surprises.

Fly Away Home lies just eight miles from the western border of southern Oregon's Umpqua National Forest, which is laced with logging roads, trails, and possible campsites. I got out my old Forest Service map and the folder of trail descriptions for the various districts, and surmised I could take Muphin and myself on a little camping adventure up-mountain, after the weather warmed, after Bethroot and I had gotten the garden planted.

The weeks passed, the days finally became more often sunny than not. We spaded the garden beds, seeded many of them with promises of Summer and Autumn green salads. When the tomato, pepper, basil, and squash plants we'd started in the coldframe were ready, they filled out the garden. Everything was thoroughly weeded and deeply mulched.

I still had the cabinet units I had built fifteen years before, for the year in my late thirties when I lived out of the back of my little '70 Datsun pickup, which I still affectionately called "Fly." Since then they had served as storage space on the trailer porch, the hinges now a little rusty, the leather closures torn, the plywood dulled and soiled. I repaired and improved, reinstalled the units in the canopied bed of the truck, tested the campstove to make sure it worked well, got extra gas, stove fuel, and other essentials on my twice-monthly trip to town.

I really didn't know what I would be capable of, what my limits were. It had been seven years since I hiked the eleven miles round-trip to the Hershberger Mountain Lookout, and that was in the company of an experienced, and indulgent, trekker. I knew I wanted to visit places to some extent a little different from the terrain of my home; I did not know what my body would be up for. I'd have to take it a day at a time. Studying the map took me on a mental cruise, meandering through a maze of roads variously designated as, in descending order, "gravelled," "improved" or "primitive." Names drew me: "Shadow Falls," "Big Squaw Mountain," the latter located at the end of a "primitive."

My focus on, and excitement about, this trip made it difficult to get to sleep at night. I'd keep going over my route and list of supplies, work to shut out negative fantasies about encountering hostile men. I was a little scared to be going alone, without another woman; I'd feel safer and worry less if there were two of us, though I knew Muphin would be an alert watch dog. She'd growl and bark furiously at any sign of intruders, make enough noise to offset her little size. Too, in those wide-awake night hours, some yearning lingered for just simply another woman to be with me, someone to love the scenery with me, someone to love me.

It rained on and off as I labored against my weather-dampened spirits to pack the truck on a day in mid-June. Because I did not want this trip to be a physical challenge when it came to food, clothing and shelter, it became a huge project to outfit myself with every conceivable comfort and convenience. In case I could find no dry kindling where I'd make camp, I packed a cardboard box from my home supply, fit it on the seat against the far door and placed a pillow on top, making a high passenger seat for Muphin who would then be able to see out the window with ease.

My mating ring disappeared during the packing; I noticed it missing from my finger late in the afternoon. I was sure it was not permanently gone; it would eventually show up somewhere in the house. But for now I was without it. I took its absence as an omen: I did not have my mate on this trip – she was not my companion, my playmate, my partner. The absence of the ring reminded me that, except for Muphin, I was alone. I would give myself this pilgrimage to experience my aloneness in a stark raw form, and determined to be content.

On the day I was to drive off, the sky was alternately blue and grey; I fretted a lot, decided again and again to start out, to stay home, to start, to stay. . . . What pushed me over the edge to get going was that I had soaked the sparse grass around the house with urine fertilizer, and the intense acrid odor was quite unpleasant. When the threat of more rain tempted me to wait a day longer and spend some time photographing the blooms in my flower beds, the stench robbed me of that excuse. Then when the sun came out again, I figured I'd just start driving, go at least the twenty minutes up to Red Top Spring, have lunch at the small lake there, and then see what happened. It was already late morning by the time I drove the dirt mile down to the county road, easing myself along with singing: "Oh, goddess, help me in my doubt, clarify my mind. . . ."

The county stops maintaining the road just two miles east from my rural delivery mailbox; from there it was a fairly steep climb up the Forest Service road through the thick stands of tall firs, cedars, and hemlocks, and the rhododendrons sprawling beneath them. Fly was more sluggish than usual with the uphill miles, which added another worry to the journey.

Lunch and a short walk beside the lake went well enough, though it was cool and often cloudy, and there was the noisy disturbance of occasional logging trucks careening around the curves on the lake road. I made myself push on from there, even though my old pickup was running poorly. Apparently the logging was happening in a different direction from the one I took, because I never encountered one of the big haulers, making my heightened state of alert driving on the winding dirt roads more tense than necessary. After wasting a lot of fuel and stress-energy coaxing along the limping truck, I finally stopped at a big turn-out and puzzled out that two of the four spark plugs were fouling out. Luckily, I had extras along in my well-stocked toolbox, and, after I exchanged them, Fly ran just fine.

It was difficult being both driver and navigator, needing eyes for the road as well as for the directions and map I had placed on the seat between me and Muphin's perch. I missed the marker for the Shadow Falls trailhead, but shortly reckoned I had gone too far and turned around, backtracked a couple miles and found the small sign and the turn-out, big enough for just one vehicle.

Though we had not travelled very many miles as the crow flies, the going had been slow, and Muphin and I were glad to be out of the truck again. She knew an honest-to-goodness hike was in store this time, and her enthusiasm led the way across a little footbridge and up the well-worn path. The description I had from the Forest Service rated the trail as "more difficult," but I didn't find it all that hard and wondered what criteria they used for their labelling. The narrow trail, just under a mile, passed through old-growth Douglas Fir, with yellow, white, and pink wildflowers in bloom along the way. It paralleled a swollen tumbling creek zigzagging its way down a nest of huge boulders, the moist path ending at a viewpoint just below the Falls. There was a bannistered stand there at the edge of the cliff, where I was engulfed by the thunder of the cascading water. While I took a few hurried photos of the scene, Muphin skirted around my feet, crept under the bannister to stand at the edge of the precipice. I gasped and begged her back; she came quickly, her steps confident and agile. It was clear she was in her element; my fear signalled the tension I was carrying more than any danger Muphin was in. On the way back to the truck I walked too fast, anxious to get to our campsite long before nightfall.

As best as I could figure it from the map, the distance from the Shadow Falls trailhead to where I intended to camp at the base of

Big Squaw Mountain was only about twenty-seven miles, but the road had more twists and turns than a handful of earthworms, and frequent potholes to add to the necessity for slow and careful driving. I spent the first seven or so miles retracing the route to where the road up from Red Top Spring had split in two; I'd take the other fork from there. Backtracking meant I was now travelling in slightly familiar territory, so I calmed down a bit, enough to think about things other than finding my way.

From the beginning, I had had anxiety about this excursion as well as excitement. At the bottom of all the negative fantasies was fear of the unknown, of being naive and thus getting myself into dangerous situations through ignorance. And fear, as well, of loneliness, and boredom. As I followed the maze of old and new logging roads I did sometimes feel lonely, ached for a companion, a playmate. Muphin was a dear friend, and I knew if I had a different perspective right then her company would be more than adequate. As the miles passed without mishap, I cheered up and relaxed, reached to Muphin for companionship, talked to her about my hopes for this trip, explained when I missed a turn. Sometimes I sang to soothe myself, which seemed to please Muphin too, as she rested on her pillow and watched the scenery.

The road numbers changed from two digits to off-shoots of four, and then to off-shoots of those which had even longer numbers, until I finally arrived at what turned out to be a mile-long overgrown track on a rocky ledge, ending at a widened area, big enough to park Fly and make a comfortable camp. There was enough dry wood lying about for a small fire later, after I'd done a little exploring. According to the trail description the trailhead should have been right at this spot, but there was no sign, no well-travelled footpath, and the brush on the slopes was thick. I pushed my way a few yards through bushes and young trees on the uphill side, and found the remains of an old, splintered cedar signpost lying near a meager suggestion of a trail, now overgrown and barely accessible. This was rather discouraging, but I figured I'd wait and see how it all looked to me in the morning. For now I was pleased and proud with the fact I had gotten myself there, and set about to make camp in earnest.

Soon I had a fire going, heated water for tea and ate the supper I had packed. The late sun defied the chill of the approaching evening as I settled in my campchair and stared at the layer upon layer of ridges stretching to the western horizon, each one capped with heavy clouds. There was a slight breeze rustling in the trees, then came other sounds that washed through the silence: strange sounds, like a woman singing, chanting, wailing – eerily, mournfully. Not loud, more as if the tones gently drifted around the huge boulders and cliff behind and above me. I turned and faced the mountain, strained to listen. Faint, elusive, then gone. Inexplicably, I was comforted, and less afraid, of both the known and the unknown.

Muphin wasn't sure she liked the camping-out scene, preferred to be in the cab of the truck instead of near the smoky fire with me. The descending sun was swallowed by huge dark clouds rising from the west, and I worried about whether they would continue my way and dump their density on my campsite and the rock cliff rising behind me. If it had to rain while I was on this expedition, I hoped it would happen only at night.

It grew too cold for comfort, but I didn't want to make a bigger fire, so the air mattress and sleeping bag I'd laid out in the back of the truck beckoned. A half dozen votive candles took the chill off my little bedroom-on-wheels. Muphin was glad to nestle into the sleeping bag with me, so I was cozy enough to read for a long while before I could shut down my mind for the night.

The sound of rain was loud on the metal roof in the dark wee hours, waking me from a sleep hardwon on the narrow mattress which had lost some of its oomph during the night. I noted the rain, affirmed it would be gone in time for the hike up the mountain, and slumbered off again. I slept lighter than I needed, awoke around 6:00, hoped the dreamy fog surrounding my hillside campsite would burn off with the rising sun, and dozed for another hour or so. But when I awoke for good it was to a drizzly day, the

ridges to the west hidden behind a thick veil of clouds that
blanketed me all around. The cliff and mighty boulder above me
were obliterated. I stayed snug in my sleeping bag with Muphin,
who had cuddled zipped in with me all night. She was definitely a
creature of comfort, could do without this rainy camping. I looked
up from my book to stare out the plastic windows at the little
nearby trees, eventually able to see beyond them to the pale ridges
as the day warmed, the clouds broke up a little, and the drizzle
stopped. When I had enough of idleness and not very comfortable
half-sitting, half-lying in the truck, I decided it was time for tea and
to brave the day. Just as I was struggling from heavy pajamas into
daytime clothes, some shadows began to appear, welcome evidence
of sunshine sifting through the thick screen of clouds. My desire to
climb the trail after breakfast was rekindled with a cup of hot tea,
and an occasional burst of warm sunlight. I sat contentedly and
watched the cliff, watched the thick mist drift across the nearest
boulder, which resembled an enormous nipple, round and dimpled
and flat on top.

With the hot tea in me and Muphin warm, and warming, on my
lap, I closed my eyes to meditate, to simply breathe, bringing all of
my being into the present, to a complete and conscious rest. I sat
this way for several minutes, loving this strand that runs through
the fabric of my life: wherever I am, I can stop and close my eyes
and breathe – fill my chest, push air deep to my belly, know what
is at the core of me: a womb-one who breathes.

While I continued to breathe deeply, I opened my eyes to my
surroundings. I had brought myself to a place I had merely seen on
a map, a place whose name drew me to her, a mountain called
Big Squaw, a woman's place. I looked up at the top of the cliff,
visible now because of the sun's work, and, after having looked at
that spot many times the evening before, I finally *saw* the woman
for the first time. She was a face, lying, profiled against the sky,
obviously a woman's face, with softly rounded cheek and chin, a
prominent nose and bold forehead. Her mouth was open as
though she were singing. I saw her face so clearly now, wondered

how I could have missed it, then remembered the singing, wailing, I had heard, and the strange sense of comfort it had given me. Someone was accompanying me on this healing quest, someone who lifted my burden of grief and carried it for me for a while.

Alas, the rain returned and Muphin and I retreated to the makeshift camper where we each ate our breakfasts as best we could in the cramped and awkward space. I had to decide whether to continue with my plans or return home. Although I would have liked to dare to climb that mountain, to touch the woman's face, the thought of continued bouts of rain and confinement made me yearn for home. I chose to be content with what I had seen and heard from Big Squaw.

When there was a slight let-up in the rain I made certain the firepit hid no embers, got my chair and pots and stowed them in the truck, and invited Muphin to her seat. I turned Fly around and followed the intersecting roads toward home, driving in and out of thundering cloudbursts, dodging flooded potholes, the pummeling rain alternating with brief patches of bright sunshine, all of it a glorious celebration of the very Beingness of things.

Just about where the gravel road became paved again, I seemed to ride out from the storm, only about three miles from my own dirt lane. For yet another mile the pavement stayed dry and I came to White Rock Road, a government logging road I knew well from all the times I had used it to get to the high spring which feeds our waterline. And I knew this road as it extended beyond the spring, climbing up and up around the ridges several miles past Buck Butte, to White Rock, where the road ended at a powdery white cliff. In the time-space of that dry mile I had decided that Muphin and I were not ready to retreat to the comforts of home; this journey was not yet over.

I needed no map for this unplanned-for side-trip, could gaze with ease at the magnificent views at each turn in the road, the great expanse of blue sky holding brilliant cotton-candy tufts. The way was familiar, the road in good repair. I traveled slowly for the pleasure of the drive, arrived at White Rock around noon, and made camp on a wide shelf, about a quarter-mile across the draw from the cliff. I felt so relaxed, safe, peaceful as I made a rock-bounded firepit, gathered some wood, ate a hearty lunch, and had a good long nap in the sun, making up for the prior night's broken sleep.

I passed a lazy afternoon at the campsite, happy with my book or just observing the sky. The silence was unbroken except for a rare high-flying airplane. I suspected there were birds whose song was beyond the limits of my short-range hearing, and wildlife I'd not see because of Muphin's presence. I cooked up an ample pre-packaged dinner on the little stove, then made a fire, just big enough to keep mosquitoes at bay, and give me a bit of warmth as I watched the sun descend to the west and then hide behind the white cliff, watched the clouds drift around the ridges to the north.

Night's approach was hastened by the appearance of a huge black cloud which soon covered the whole area except for a slit on the northern horizon, where there was yet some pale grey and gold from the setting sun. Muphin and I were already settled in Fly by then, and I glanced out the windows occasionally to see the black cover on the dimming pot. My full belly, the growing darkness, and the warmth of the sleeping bag brought on a good night's sleep.

I would not have been surprised by a rainfall during the night, but there was none. Instead, by morning, the cloud had turned into a dense white fog, rendering hopeless my intention of photographing the white cliff just as the sunrise kissed it. But I was good-natured about it, satisfied with whatever the goddess would give me. And she gave me much.

The fog lifted soon after I got up, small tufts of it swirling around the ridges, falling into the draw, then up again to be evaporated by the sun. I sat on my chair with my tea and watched the soft quiet aerodynamics, sometimes caught up in the show myself as a thin cloud swirled around me. Muphin curled asleep on my lap when I sat cross-legged on a large stump to meditate. Open-eyed, gazing at the white cliff, I smiled to discover the juxtaposition of the curved lines of the cliff, and the narrow road ending in front of it, formed gigantic eyes. There was a woman there, her left eye held closed, winking at me. A very playful, trickster goddess, who had obviously been watching me since I arrived.

Twice I walked up the brushy slope above my camp with my little shovel to dig a shallow hole and deposit my body's waste into the welcoming earth. Then a simple breakfast of fruit and nuts and a couple of rye crackers before I wandered on the sloping meadow with my camera, Muphin always close by.

This was not a natural meadow, really, but nature's response to a clear-cut, filling in the shaven terrain with countless rhododendron bushes now in full pink bloom. Coarse grasses, wildflowers, and many little green plants almost completely hid the charred remnants of the burned slash. Beyond the meadow stood an evergreen forest, the edge of the trees forming a sharp east-west line which only a managerial intent would create. But within the forest the early sunlight filtered through the branches to large areas of rambling rhodies, their pink and green vivid against the deep brown trunks of the firs and the dark shade amongst the trees. Muphin, who preferred nonstop exploration with me in tow, patiently waited for me when I stopped to set up my tripod and with studied care attempted perfect portraits of the flowers.

Intending to return home by morning's end, I secured all my gear in Fly, then decided to drive over to the cliff, to stroke the face of the winking goddess before I left. I was glad I did, for the view east from there was a grand expanse of ridges many miles away, with four mountaintops graced with patches of snow. I sat bare-chested on a log in the hot sun, my spirit fed by the enormity of the scene. Presently an orange-shafted flicker gave me staccato conversation from atop a high blackened stump, then swooped and flitted down and across the draw, settling on a fir. Then a raven appeared, cawing, from the forest and drifted toward me and the cliff. I twisted my head up and around to watch her climb high and out of sight. Rhododendrons bloomed behind me, some of the flowers perfectly framed by the rock wall. So much beauty, and so liberally given, love lavished upon me by everything I saw and heard. I lay back upon the log and, impassioned by the pink blooms, the sky, the birds, the mountains, I stroked myself to a joyful singing orgasm. Muphin came from her resting place in the shade beneath a bush to lick my throaty breathing, washed my whole face, then lay quietly above my head on the log.

I lacked no lover in this scene: she was present everywhere. I was complete, and content.

The sun reached zenith, reflected with dazzling brightness off the white cliff; heat shimmered in the air. Both Muphin and I needed to leave the sun's intensity, were ready to be homeward bound. Before turning onto the descending road I pulled Fly back onto the shelf where I had camped, from where I could see the playful eyes. I winked back at her, then began the easy drive home.

"Gender Studies"

The early morning sun dappled the log where she stood, just outside the poultry fencing which protects my flower beds from her scratching. Just as I was finishing the tall glass of spring water, to break the long night's fast, I had been drawn to the back porch by a sound that could only be the crowing of a rooster. But we no longer have roosters in our small flock of hens, having learned many years ago cocks tend to be quarrelsome at best, often vicious, not to mention lasciviously bothersome to the hens. No place for them on this Lesbian land!

So who could be greeting the sun with such a hoarse guttural song? I didn't see her as I scanned the area around the hen house, but then I heard it again, definitely a crowing, though a somewhat more gentle rendition of the sound that years ago would crack the early morning silence and end my dreams. My ears directed me to the source of this oddity: a hen fluffed her grey-and-black striped feathers as she faced the sun filtering through the trees on the eastern slope, jutted out her head with its hen-size bright red comb, and called with true purpose and seeming delight. I kept still, listening and watching. She knew I was there. Indeed, she seemed to welcome me witnessing her ritual. She "crowed" again, with wing-beat accompaniment, and then stood still, as though listening for response, or perhaps she meditated in repose.

I realize, now, that I have heard this song before, coming even later in the day as the hens range for their daily bounty on the brushy hillside or in the soft earth down in the orchard. I've looked up from my work down in the garden and listened with curiosity

and amusement. Maybe this morning's Barred Rock has a reper-
toire of time and place, or perhaps the hens pass this queenly
function around among themselves. Clearly, they, like I, need no
male in their midst to herald the dawn, or announce abundance, or
just celebrate being alive. We all sing our own songs.

Reflections

I

The half-slice moon
startles the early night sky.
My chest rises to the occasion
warms the crisp Winter air with song:
"Oh, goddess of the moon and stars above,
shine your everlasting love on me."
I heave the sound loud and sweet
wrap the trees and fill the valley
with the fullness of my singing.
Again and again I call the prayer.
My lungs swell and empty
swell and empty
my throat an ever easier conduit.
The moon and I
please each other
with our reflections.

II

The moon has followed her light to the west
disappeared beyond the trees
shines by now on a far distant Pacific wave.
A sampling of our garden's harvest
has simmered all day on the woodstove

biscuits rise in the oven.
Muphin, startled by unordinary sound,
sets to barking.
I listen, and as she grows quiet,
begin to hear another's song.
A woman sings high and lilting notes.
Her long melody
sweetly threading through the forest
finds welcome in my kitchen.
My land partner
at her new house in process
way up the hill
must be warming some Winter air too.
Her music draws a smile from me,
so glad to hear her too-infrequent song.

III

I reach gently with leftover biscuits:
"I liked your singing last night."
        "Oh? . . . I heard *you* . . . but I didn't sing."
"But you must have, after the moon had set.
Muphin heard you first, and barked."
        "Now, let me see . . . last night. . . .
        No, I am certain I did no singing."
A song without a singer?
In truth, I'd likely not hear
notes sent down the hill.
I barely hear a bellowing hoot
trying, and often failing, for my attention.

But I heard a woman singing.

IV

The night the moon shone half her face
and pulled full voice from me
a woman I have loved long and deep
sang in concert on a distant stage.
Did her song find its way
through mountains and valleys
and years
to visit once again this southern hill
where we loved
and sang together
long ago?

Or did the moon
in wise reflection
as she dipped toward the sea
bend my calling back to me?

Goddess
to goddess
to goddess . . .
in everlasting love.

Chant in first stanza composed by Sarah Tames.

Weeding at Dawn

It all began with a bag of calendula seeds, culled from a friend's garden. I had so admired the bright orange and yellow blooms, coveted a bed of them for my hillside. So I asked for some seed on a day when I was admiring flowers but forgetting about the care they would require. And so, a few months later, came a bag of seeds; must have been at least two cups of them, which is a lot of potential calendula plants, and each plant a potential mother for a myriad of offspring. No small corner of an already established bed would do . . . I had a new project on my hands.

I have this problem about not being able to just simply dispose of too-many seeds, or plants, or cuttings. . . . It has taken me years to learn the vegetable plants will be healthier and more prolific if I thin out the seedlings at least approximating the spacings suggested by the gardening books. (Even so I keep a rather crowded vegetable garden.) So I do try to plant fewer seeds to begin with, saving them for the next year, and pull the excess in the beds for my supper salads and the pleasure of the hens.

But those calendula seeds wanted planting, so I set to work on a weedy, brushy spot at the bottom of the (weedy, ferny) lawn just below the house. Like all the rest of the seventeen beds which claim the slope that is my flower garden, this one too would have to be wrested from thick roots of wild honeysuckle, blackberries, and poison oak, as well as tall grass and weeds of many shapes and habits. And the remaining soil would require wheelbarrow loads of compost brought from the composting privy up the hill and off toward the east side of the land. And then there'd be digging it all in. . . .

In truth, my work load really did not need another flower bed, especially when I thought of all the constant weeding this bed at the edge of wildness would need, to keep the calendula from being engulfed by the original denizens of the place. So I made an agreement with myself: I'd dig and clear and haul and dig again and plant, and then let nature take her course. I'd give the calendula a good birth and hope they would be hardy enough to live and bloom amidst whoever came to accompany them.

And so the "wild bed," as I called it, was added to the plots terracing the hillside. This one was set well apart from the carefully tended others, where roses, dahlias, poppies, irises, lilies, gladioli, mums, peonies, daisies, azaleas, hydrangeas, rhododendrons . . . please my amateur gardener's attempt at an elegant country garden. I told myself this wild bed would receive no additional mulch or compost, though I would of course give it plenty of water in the Summer months.

The calendula did thrive, adding bright orange and yellow to the grey days of late Winter, and joined with the red, pink, purple, burgundy of other flowers on the hill to celebrate the long awaited early Spring. But they were indeed, by the second year, neighbored up to their stems by countless other growing things which seemed determined to occupy every inch of soil where the calendula had not yet done their hoped-for spread. It looked like there might not be any spread at all, so pressing were the weeds. I looked at the calendula . . . and I looked at the roses, the peonies, the poppies. . . . I saw what could happen if I put my hands and little trowel among the infant seedlings.

Oh no! Yet another bed to tend, and I had promised. . . .

*   *   *

It has been an unusually cold and wet Spring this year, but some early mornings the sun warms the treetops to gold when I get up at 6:00 or so. I drink my glass of spring water, bid a good morning to the hens as I let them out of their house for the day, and take myself to the so-called wild bed. Sometimes I take my trowel with me, sometimes not; sometimes I grab a pair of gardening gloves from my garden bucket; some days a jacket is needed against the morning chill. In any case, I have come to the wild bed to start the day, when there is a silence lying like a soft cloud on the land, with not even the birds having much to say as yet. I kneel at the edge of the bed and work the weeds up by their roots, careful not to disturb the wanted calendula plants. I step mindfully into the bed and squat, following the runners of sorrel to their mother plants, tug at ferns, excavate young blackberry vines coming from the still-hidden ancient roots.

I do all this without a sense of accomplishing a chore; it has nothing to do with the list of work I keep and follow through most days. "Weed the wild bed" never appears on that list, so it never gets crossed off. Would I put "meditate" on a list? Or "do Tai Chi"? Or "sit and stare at the ridges and think"? Like these things I so love to do, and which deepen my days and bind them together like the drone of a chant, I weed in the wild bed at dawn and weed myself, blessed by the simplicity of soil and plants, morning dew and a quiet sky. The sun floats higher . . . her rays dress the lengths of firs on the west side of the orchard by the time I stand and breathe deeply, the fresh crisp air cleansing my body, my mind.

Clock

Sand drops
grain by grain
through the thin life-glass.
Each fading petal
each new bud:
a tiny rock of time-counting.
I see time
in the texture of my skin
in the changing colors of my hair
  the leaves
     Muphin's furry coat.
A spider
smaller than the new brown spot
on my wrinkled hand
hurriedly climbs the long, long road
of my thigh.
The sand drops
records the spinner's progress
and my own
while we travel this lifetime
and I breathe an ever-slower rhythm.

Scrap

Sarah, my sister, and I worked hard for many days of her annual two week August visit. She flies the whole way from Connecticut, she claims, for the sheer pleasure of helping me get in my firewood for the following Winter, and eating her fill of the healthy vegetables we grow. Before we got to the firewood this year, however, we had a great time building a fine roof over my woodshed, that large space among the tall cedars and firs which shelters the dry cordwood near my house. The stacks were previously covered each year with huge sheets of torn and patched black plastic I had to wrestle with every time I needed to bring wheelbarrow loads into the house. What an improvement to have them gone! When the roof construction was finished, we got to the loading and hauling of the firewood.

Big Blue, our workhorse of a farm truck, was already getting to be a rusty relic when my land partner and I got her as part of the purchase agreement for this land. Each year we coax her to haul overfilled loads of gravel for our road from the quarry twenty-five miles away, slambang her way up the old logging tracks into the upper forest where we cut up the fallen dead madrones, haul the loads of leaves we rake from our mile and a quarter road, crawl in reverse – her bed bulging with firewood – down the narrow slope to my woodshed, make runs to the county dump, fetch lumber and drums of kerosene from town, and generally move everything around on this land which is too big or awkward for our smaller vehicles. And each year I cross my fingers for Big Blue to see us through another year, hopefully another decade, before she might grow beyond repair and be banished to a junk yard.

This year Sarah and I loaded and unloaded Big Blue six times to move and stack a winter's supply of fuel for the big woodstove that warms my round house. We worked well together, each loving the play of muscles and rhythm as we handed the many hundreds of pieces one to the other. Sometimes we talked about the joys and sorrows of our childhoods, when we were ten years apart in an unhappy family (I the older sister and the middle child of three), or about our current lives with the continent between us; but often we worked in a verbal near silence, with an occasional grunt to ease a heft, or one's burst of laughter at another's wit. We worked ourselves to sweaty exhaustion day after day, rewarded by hot solar-warmed showers, the garden's abundance, pies and cookies from my oven, sweet conversation, and sound sleeping.

Half way through our second week together, it was time for a break from arduous labor. We decided to take a mid-afternoon walk down our gravel road, flanked on both sides by forest thick with evergreens and some maples, chinkapins, and a few alders, with manzanita hugging the banks here and there. We walked slowly, talked gently, soothing the tender spots we each carried after a painful misunderstanding we'd had earlier in the visit, and the work we had done to heal from it. As blood sisters we have some sensitivities in common, both having learned some defensive strategies growing up in a family that felt more often than not like a war-zone. And as loving and self-nurturing adults we are each committed to honest and careful communication. So we walked and let defenses fall away, like the madrone leaves which blanketed the sides of the road and filled the ditches, beckoning to yet another project awaiting me in the coming weeks.

During the decades after the last of the original big homesteading family had left this hilltop and no one lived up here, the road saw infrequent use. Now and again someone apparently did drive a pickup out from town and up the abandoned road to dump a derelict kitchen appliance off the side of the track and down the forested bank. Over the years some small sections of the forest became graveyards of rusting metal. Sarah and I spied one such place as we ambled. I had been wanting a closer look at those discarded parts of other people's lives I have noticed as I drive by, so we wandered down a deer path crisscrossing the bank, and poked about among the debris. I found the top of an old top-loading washing machine lying near the bottom of an even older wringer washer, as though to chronicle the advance of technology for a homemaker's relative ease. Nearby lay the bare springs of perhaps a car seat, and scattered about were metal stove doors, drawers and hinges, and pieces whose function was no longer decipherable. All were in various states of decay, some pieces still semi-intact under the thick white enamel coating, others turning to flaky rust in the process of being swallowed by the voracious earth.

I found one particularly fascinating piece, about as big as the pan that catches the pie drippings in my oven. I held it up to the light filtering through the trees and saw it was a work of beautiful rusty lace, with holes dotting the entire surface, the whole piece flimsily held together by metal worked and softened by oxidation, the breath of the earth the lacemaker. I saw in it the story of ore mined from the soil, processed and worked into sheets of steel and fashioned into the panels of a cookstove, or the round barrel of a washing machine. I saw, too, a woman laboring with such tools to cook and clean for her family (or maybe *with* her Lesbian lover?). And as surely as these implements of her trade were returning to their origins, she no doubt had by now felt the breath of death herself, and was somewhere becoming a bony lace. I felt a quiet reverence for her, and her work, and for the magnificent patience of the goddess as she takes what is discarded, what is no longer needed, and accepts it into her timeless bounty.

My sister and I studied this forest history together, enacting a playmating we rarely shared as children, when I struggled as a Lesbian teenager against all the social and religious pressures that made me an invisible misfit; and she, the baby of the family, often felt like an only child, ineffectual and suffocated by our parents' quarreling. We did not have the friendship those thirty or so years ago which we were making now, as we prowled around the rusting cast-offs from unknown homes, artifacts suggesting stories we assumed might resemble our own. We played into a widening trust between us, learning to scrap the worn-out parts of a mutual legacy we have no need of anymore.

Our walk continued on the road and off onto side tracks where Sarah nuzzled moss-covered logs with her fingertips, and we both feigned grief over empty fairy cups. The afternoon grew late, so we headed back to the house, stopping at the newly-roofed woodshed to admire our handiwork and exchange yet another round of "thank-you" and "you're-welcome."

As we passed over the short ramp that leads onto the front porch, Sarah stopped to notice the dilapidated high-top moccasins resting in the flower beds on either side of the ramp, wanted to know their story. I explained I had originally found them in a San Francisco garbage can about twenty-two years before, around the time when she came west to see me for the first time, when she was just twenty and actively heterosexual, and I hadn't even yet dreamed of country living. The mocs had been relegated to the trash, no doubt, because of the worn-through holes in the softened leather sole. When I found them the uppers were still thick and sturdy, identified as buffalo hide many years later at the shoe repair shop where I had them resoled with hard rubber for the third and last time. The hide, lined with sheep's fleece, came up high enough to cover my ankles. I spent many an Oregon Winter on this land with my feet warmed by those sturdy soft wrappings.

When that third sole wore through and the fleece had thinned to only a few remaining hairs, it was time to retire the moccasins. But I couldn't just cast them back into a garbage can. I wanted to honor their years of service as well as the life and death of the animals whose skin had warmed my feet. And I wanted to watch the slow process of decay and transformation, to witness the animal become the soil. So they sit as sentries beneath the two sword ferns bordering the entrance to my house.

Sarah listened to my tale intently, then we walked arm-in-arm, our feet passing between the weather-kneaded leather, each knowing the poignant difference between abandonment and letting go, the sweetness of growing old enough to learn love.

Egg Song

The song of a hen when she has just laid an egg is unmistakable. A deep-chested cackle crescendos to a head-top screech, a stuttering of syllables repeating and repeating, a song I interpret as filled with triumph and joy, and not a little humor.

So when I heard the black hen on my way down the path to the Poogoda, heard her singing her egg song and saw her strutting there at the edge of the forest, I suspected there may be reason other than the high heat for the paucity of eggs in the hen house nests on these mid-Summer mornings. As I approached, having a rather urgent appointment at the outhouse, the hen scuttled away, but I heard other feet shuffling in the leaves just down the bank from the path. I interrupted my stride just enough to spy one of our red hens emerging from beneath some brush. She did not announce her presence, or sing of accomplishment, with the gusto the black had, but quietly ambled off among the trees. I made a mental note to come back later and investigate the spot.

I forgot about that sleuthing I wanted to do, got caught up in the heavy load of seasonal work. A few mornings later, when I again found zero eggs in the nests, testifying to either the discomfort or recalcitrance of eight hens, I remembered the strutting hen and her loud celebration. I had noted the location on the path, opposite from a small cedar which has grown up in the midst of what must have been a logging track many years ago, so the suspect nest was easy to find. The bank there is steep and I hadn't bothered to change into sturdy shoes, so I slipped and slid among the low branches, and held onto the tree trunks as I made my way the ten or so feet down to the bush where I had spied the red hen.

I remember when I was young enough to still believe in the benevolence of magical beings, in tooth fairies and gifting elves. I'd awake in the morning to find a coin had replaced a tooth, fallen out the day before and placed beneath my pillow when I went to bed, with assurances from my mother the fairy would take the tooth and leave me a gift. And, oh! the thrill of sneaking down the stairs on Christmas morning, to be amazed that a tree had somehow grown overnight in a corner of the living room, a tree covered with shiny colored balls and tinsel, brightly wrapped packages lying beneath it. Years later the fairies and elves would work their magic with my first woman-lover's lips. There too, the excitement of discovery, the exploding pleasure of surprise.

Now the thrill was no less keen as I gently pulled the brush aside and discovered a clutch of ten eggs in a shallow leafy nest, rounded and smoothed by the hens' home-making. As we have no rooster in the flock, I knew these eggs had no birthing destiny, so I carefully lifted each one and placed them in a cradle made by pulling up my shirt, and carried them to the house. While my own cackling bears no resemblance to the hens', I match my joy to theirs, and am truly grateful for their song.

Cellar Journal

I drove Big Blue to Bargain Lumber today, taking the county roads along the seasonally low South Umpqua River, then through Dillard and Winston and back toward the freeway to the road which sidles it. The Interstate is no place for Blue. The speed of the back roads is enough of a challenge for her twenty-eight years, though her loose steering makes the curves of the county roads rather unsettling. But caution made the thirty or so miles of scenery pass slowly enough for me to really enjoy it, with no traffic to keep up with, no potential passers to look out for. Muphin nestled beside me on the wide seat, her fuzzy chin occasionally resting on my thigh as I guided the big truck along the back country route. I drove by pastures dotted with grazing cattle, apple trees laden with a full harvest, the mountains of sawdust occupying a few acres at the vast lumber mill, homes and small stores, a modest shopping center. And the river. I've never seen it so low. (Do I say this every year?) Rocks stand like the nobs on dotted-swiss material, shallow pools look almost stagnant where water rushes in other seasons. The honest-to-goodness rain we finally had the other day, after the Summer's drought, seems to have given a boost to the center of the flow, and a little white shows on the leading edges around the rocks.

I reached the lumber yard in good time, the chill of the morning not quite burnt away by the nooning sun. I had gone prepared to have to spend $140 for fourteen sheets of 3/8 inch plywood, but worked my way through their pile of used, reject sheets and came away with twenty-two pieces at $2 each. A ratty lot to be sure, but there will be enough good wood to do the job I have in mind, after I saw off the ragged edges and cover up some holes. More work than using new sheets, but far less money, and I am pleased with my scrounging.

The job this plywood is destined for is the storage cellar I aim to build under my house. Now that I have completed the project of putting the shakes on the exterior of the house, a year in the doing and seventeen years on my mind, I shall one day soon begin this next, and probably last, major change to my home. There is no clear and present need for this addition; the gatehouse out by the road still serves as storage for canned goods and apples, empty suitcases and boxes, tools, motor oil, the bee-keeping equipment no longer used since the hives died, odds and ends too numerous to name, or remember. But I have had this idea for a few years now that I want to build something on the wedge-shaped cement slab which lies beneath the kitchen area, where my dodecagonal nest rises high over the slope it is built on.

I know there is more in this than merely wanting to use that cement slab, and I certainly don't need another project. I see myself pulling in, gathering my resources closer around myself. As Bethroot's new house nears completion I feel our mutual independence getting clearer and more complete as well. At fifty-five, I want more autonomy, more a sense of being whole in my own private space, the first I've had in twenty-six years. And who knows the future of the gatehouse. Will someone else come to live there some year? I don't want to have to suddenly take all my stuff out of there some day because the space is needed for some other woman's expansion. I'd rather build new storage space for myself now, when I am doing it so specifically for me.

Going for the plywood today was a commitment to the job, to taking this next step in my singular home-making. As I drove the miles back through the countryside I felt excited, ready to begin. I pushed Big Blue gently along the river, passed deciduous trees just turning on their Autumn colors, and flower gardens bright with marigolds and petunias, mums and dahlias. The river was a peaceful companion as we both wound our way to our destinies, she to the sea, and I to the land of my *Fly Away Home*. As I rounded a bend I noticed a large bird standing motionless on a rock, the water eddying around her. I slowed and pulled off the road onto a wide shoulder, asked Muphin to wait, and walked back along the road to where I could see the Great Blue Heron just as she took off from the rock and soared away from me above the river. I stood unmoving, hoping she'd come back. As though she heard my hope, she banked and curved her way back upriver, swooping over the water, her great wings undulating in a slow beating of her medium, her legs stretched out long beyond her tail. My eyes followed her as she passed in front of me then continued above the water's trail. She had gone about fifty yards when another Heron I hadn't noticed took off from the river's edge and the two of them flew beyond my seeing. Independent in their fishing, harmonious in their flight – I took them for an omen.

Wednesday, October 12

Yesterday I did the excavation for the cellar. A young couple started this house in the early 70's but didn't finish it before their marriage fell apart, he left, and she eventually put the house and forty acres up for sale. They had worked hard, probably too hard, to reclaim the old abandoned homestead in the three and a half years they were here. They tore down old buildings and built new, developed a spring and laid a mile-long water pipe, almost finished a massive wooden water tank, fenced in and maintained a large garden, and more, while they both held jobs in town. They completed the frame of the house, got the insulation, windows, and most of the flooring installed, the roof on. I don't know what they had in mind for the cement slab they took great care to pour precisely between foundation posts, matching the shape of the pie section of the house above it. They had to dig the hard soil from the gentle slope to make a flat area extending eight feet into the hill. To make possible the construction I have planned, I had to cut the clay bank back further, which turned out to be hard physical labor.

The clay surrounding the cement slab is extremely hard-packed. I used the heavy broad pickax and shovel, took out at least six wheelbarrow loads of beige dirt, some of it in large clumps, about as hard as decomposed granite. I worked to cut the clay bank back far enough so there will be enough space to work in, either to hammer or drill, when I go to attach the plywood to the outside of the walls. And in the process of picking and shovelling I understood I should make the clearance between the walls and the bank wide enough to allow a hoe or broom in there to keep the space clean. I can tell from the buildup around the additional foundation posts we installed seventeen years ago that the clay crumbles and migrates, and would eventually fill in this space and cause damage to the walls. So I had to do more excavation than I had planned, and my arms and back were sore by the end of the afternoon. I'll be glad I put out the extra effort. I really want to do this project right, want the cellar to work: stay cool and dry in all seasons, and last for many decades.

Yesterday as I worked at the base of the yew post that supports one of the twelve corners of the house, and which is destined to become a corner for the cellar, I came upon a large reddish root in the path of the cleanout space I was making. About one and a half inches in diameter, it would make the task of pulling dirt through with a hoe difficult. Figuring I had to cut it out, I dug away the clay around it and discovered it appeared to be attached to the post! Not just attached, like some barnacle clinging for security, but seemingly *growing* from the post itself. The woman we bought this land from told us these unmilled posts extend six feet into the ground, without any concrete reinforcement, yew wood purported to be as strong as iron, its heart virtually indestructible. It looks like this post decided to simply relocate its life from whatever forest it was shorn, sending out at least this one big root into the clay hill my house is built upon. I wonder if there are yet more tentacles reaching out into the dry soil in those six feet below the surface, and if the other posts have done the same. There is no visible sign, at least not to my arboreally untrained eye, of any other attempt at new life: no little green sprig inching out from the trunk, no increase of the diameter or height that would warp the beams attached to it.

I decided to leave the root, no matter the obstacle it would prove to my cleaning. I'd let the small difficulty it caused me be an exchange for the inspiration of its tenacity, its determination to continue its purpose no matter what, and endure.

Friday, October 14

Late evening, soon to bed. I am weary from many hours of hard work. This morning I worked on the cellar, still installing the 2″ × 6″ top plates under the joists, which required my hammering three-and-a-half-inch long 16d nails up over my head, against gravity's inclination. Plus I had to chisel notches in the iron-like yew posts to receive these boards. And I'll have to chisel them again because I have understood I do have to install 2″ × 4″s under those top plates in order for the outside wall of plywood to have a nailing surface. So there is more work in this stage than I had realized, and more lumber required than I had counted for. I must use the lumber I have very carefully, frugally, so I don't end up having to buy any. I am recycling boards from the old trailer porch and the wooden water tank, whose floor rotted out before it could be put to use. I love using this old stuff, both because of the savings and for the pleasure of making do with what I already have.

I had a mishap this morning which could have caused serious injury. I was trying to install one of those 2″ × 6″s when it fell down onto my face, clobbering my chin. As there were four 16d nails sticking out of it, I shudder to think what could have happened to my face, my eyes. . . . As it is I have a lump and a little broken skin on my chin, sore to be sure, but I consider myself fortunate. I had to stop working and moan for a while, holding to my chin first the offending board, and then the cold blade of the big timber-framing chisel. All this worked to quell the pain in my chin, but my neck and shoulders ached badly. I finished the installation, and caulked the small spaces left, then figured it was time for an already very late lunch. Soon after I stopped working, I realized how tired and sore I was, enough to make returning to more of the same work at the cellar not a good idea for today.

Julie, who knows a lot about trees, was here yesterday, working on Bethroot's new house. I joined them for supper up there last evening and described the mysterious root seemingly growing out of the yew post. Julie asked a few questions and, upon learning the root is reddish in color and, yes, there is a cedar nearby, about twenty feet away, she suggested it is probably a root from that cedar. So instead of imagining the process of this yew post sprouting new life below ground, I now play a movie in my mind of the cedar reaching through the earth in search of nutrients, perhaps to the water so liberally sprinkled on the lawn on the far side of the house. She pushes her tentacle through the hard-packed clay, winding around others' roots perhaps, and collides with the immovable post. I can just imagine her resting there a moment (a day? a year?), deciding what to do in the face of this obstacle.

I remember the chant-story we did at Summer camp when I was a kid, about the lion hunt. We mimed our way under and over and around obstacles, undaunted in pursuit of an imaginary quarry. Now here is this cedar, her root on a water-hunt and she comes smack-dab up against the hardest plant growing hereabouts. She can't go through it, and for some reason I can't fathom, she doesn't go 'round it. So she dives down beside it, hugging the edge of the trunk so closely I had thought the root emanated from the post rather than joined it from a different source. I wonder what story of their companionship lies deeper below the surface, what twists and turns the cedar root makes around the yew post, whether indeed the root travels all six feet to the bottom of the

post and from there starts up again in search of the thirst-quench-
ing shallows some fifteen or so feet further down the slope.

With all this in mind, I looked at that cedar today, her branches
heavy with last night's rain. She is not an awfully old tree, younger
than the firs who stand wider and taller around her. There in the
line of the deer fencing which encircles my house and protects my
flower beds, she is not particularly eye-catching. Having discovered
what is most likely her tenacious root these 20 feet away, I feel a
deeper knowing and respect for her, as though I have been taken
into her confidence, privy to some intimacy in her life.

Thursday, October 20

One wall is up! Quite an accomplishment, considering the
challenges: there are no square corners, I am having to fit plywood
up against the uneven surface of the posts, no two measurements
for stud placements are the same, I am working with old used
materials, and I am doing all this with hand tools, with help from
my battery-operated drill. I have chiseled and sawed, and chiseled
and sawed some more, and caulked every possible crack that would
admit insects or mice. Today I had to do some more sculpting of
two of the posts with the chain saw, trying to get the surface as
plumb as possible to make the nearest stud sit as close to the post
as its tapered shape will allow.

My arms are weary after three continuous days at this project (I
took a day off to do town errands on Monday). I am working my
body very hard: my hands and arms with the chiseling and sawing
and setting screws and nails, my legs with the kneeling and
squatting and frequent ups and downs. At the end of the day,
which comes when it is too dark to see the small marks on the
measuring tape or the lines I have drawn, I use my last bit of
energy to clean up the saw dust, put my tools away, cover up the
stack of plywood, stash the saw horses where they won't get wet if
it should rain . . . and take a few minutes to admire my progress,
to delight in the accomplishment.

I've been trying to keep the space cleaned up as I go along, piling the board ends safely out of tripping way, keeping my tools organized so I can find what I need, sweeping the concrete slab as dust accumulates, especially after running the chain saw. When I started in on this construction last week, the floor had worn a covering of clay dust from over eighteen years of exposure. I swept more than once before the rough texture and dull grey color of the concrete bore the light of day. When the prior owners laid the concrete they did a just-adequate job, good enough for the purpose I shall make of it. They must not have been able to protect the newly poured mix from passersby, because I found a trail of a small cat's paws embedded in the floor. I thought immediately of Missy Moonshine, with her fluffy tri-colored coat and manx-like tail, who greeted me on my troubled first night on this land, and who walked in companionship with Bethroot and me for many years.

As I sweep the concrete I pay special attention to the paw prints and like to think they were made by Missy Moonshine. I am building a storage cellar where she left her signature, her steps with me even now as I begin a new life in this house which has become solely mine.

Wednesday, October 26

I finished the exterior of the third wall today, so now these three outside walls are ready to be painted with a stain, though I'm not sure when I'll accomplish that task. According to the directions on the label, it's supposed to be at least 50° when the stain is applied, and remain so for a little while. Actually, today it was warm enough, so perhaps I'll tackle the job yet this week, if I can take myself away from the carpentering. I want to get this third wall insulated and its interior plywood put on, then do the front wall and build the door, all within the next couple of weeks. I am working at this project long hours day after day, with a break here and there to take care of other things, including my need to remember I am more than a carpenter!

Like today, for example.

I had worked so painstakingly getting plywood to fit up against the posts. This morning I must have devoted two hours on a piece 76 inches long, 5 inches wide at the top, narrowing to an inch and a half at the bottom. I cut and planed and rasped it to fit up to the yew post as snug as I could get it. The air was very muggy and I sweated in the layers of shirts the cold earlier morning had warranted. Each time I worked the wood to make a better fit I told myself I could just let it be good enough, but when a little space yet showed between the plywood and the curve of the yew I took it back to the sawhorses and tried again. So the time went by, I took off my sweatshirt, and I strived for perfection. The result is a corner only another carpenter, or an artist, would truly appreciate. I look at it, at the flow of wood against wood, at the adapting of one to complement the other, and I see evidence of some of who I am. I am a woman who will work tedious hours to achieve something beautiful to my eyes, and I may be the only one who ever even notices. So I do this for myself, and for the chance that maybe someone else will see it and be pleased.

There was still the corner at the other end of the wall to fit, though that one was not so difficult. Then the pieces in between required careful adjustments. By the time I finally had the wall finished, around 5:00 p.m., I figured I had come to a good stopping place, both in terms of the work and my energy, even though it was not yet the usual 6:00 or 7:00 quitting time, when the light fades. But my hands had enough of wood and wanted soil, so I called Muphin to join me and we went off to the garden. The beds of overwintering carrots and beets have done well since I planted the seeds several weeks ago, and have needed my attention. I weeded and thinned and transplanted and watered, taking the same care with the tiny plants as I am taking with the precise measuring and cutting of wood. Then I harvested: carrots and beets still from the Summer's bounty, volunteer spinach I welcomed and tended last month, kale, mustard, parsley, two kinds of lettuce. I have been too concentrated on the cellar to replenish my larder and have gone without fresh greens for several days. This evening's salad was reward for the work of late Summer's planting, and sustenance for the work I do now.

Friday, October 28

Nearly 9:00 p.m. as I sing an audible yawn. I aim for bed soon, already changed into my flannel pajamas after a hot bath, made possible by the solar-heated tank of water on the roof, supplemented by the large kettles of water which heated all afternoon on the woodstove. I've been looking forward to that bath all week and just today made sure it happened. I took off my heavy tool belt when the light and my energy faded, put all the equipment in their right places, tarped over the remaining few pieces of plywood, and brought inside those tools I protect from the dampness. In the next days I will clean my house and take care of other chores I've been neglecting, make two potluck dishes, go to a gathering at Liz's Whispering Oaks, the newest land in our southern Oregon Lesbian community, attend Writers' Group, host our Hallowmas Gathering here on Monday, recover from that and put gravel on the road on Tuesday, go to town for errands on Wednesday. So it will not be until next Thursday when I can return to the cellar. I said good-by for a while to this project on which I have spent long, arduous, and satisfying days.

Starting with a shovel and pickax over two weeks ago, I have graduated to saws and chisels, hammer and drill . . . and the walls have gone up, the insulation in, the cracks stuffed with oakum and caulked. I still have three panels to install, two of them already cut. So the end of making the enclosure draws near. Then I get to make a door.

In all this process I knew the day would come when the task I kept putting off would have to be done: splicing into the wiring already under the house to make a path for sunlight to get to a lamp on the ceiling of the cellar. Of the many hats I wear on this land, electrician is not one I feel very comfortable in. I really don't understand electricity. I read the explanations in the books and it all still sounds mysterious to me, enough to make me wary of doing something so bold as cutting into those heavy wires which Osima hooked up when she installed the solar-electrical system for me a few years ago. I didn't even watch her do all that at the time, since I was so busy with the farm work and visitors. So here I was this morning with a small roll of wire, various sizes of wire nuts, a switch box and switch, a ceiling fixture and some sketchy instructions of how to proceed.

After making certain I had pulled the right fuse servicing the circuit I intended to cut into (other lamps on the same circuit didn't function as a result), I loaded my toolbelt with pliers, wirestripper, screwdriver, electrical tape, in addition to the usual carpenter's assortment of tools. It took some tugging on the thick, stiff 10 gauge wire, unbending it here and there to give enough slack so I could join a third line into both the color-coded hot and ground wires. I stripped the wires, joined them with the wire nuts, fed the new thinner hot red wire to the wall switch box where I attached it to the switch, then out again to the lamp fixture which received both the hot wire and the ground at its designated terminals. I had to add a $2'' \times 4''$ to the joist to provide enough surface for the fixture to hang from. All this went easily, much like following a recipe, with all the ingredients at hand and mixing together in a logical fashion. A dyke electrician who visited last Spring from England taught me it is important to test the security of a wirenut splice by pulling on the wires: if they come out then it wasn't a good connection. All my splices passed the test so I wrapped them amply with the shiny black tape. When all was in place, and I was as certain as I knew how to be that I had done everything right, I went back into the house and reinstalled the fuse. I have a bunch of 12 volt DC light bulbs, 25 watts, and took one of them back down to the cellar with me, screwed it into the fixture, and flipped the switch on the wall.

It's one thing not to understand electricity, but surely magic to stand in the light of a bulb whose glow originates in the sun shining on the photovoltaic panels on my roof. One of those chores I must get to in the coming days is to go up there and adjust the panels to their Hallowmas-to-Candlemas position, where they will greet the angle of the Winter sun to their best advantage. While electricity is an enigma to me, I feel almost worshipful as I tend to this quarterly chore. I think of the sun goddesses, like Amaterasu who conceals herself in the earth for part of each year, and only comes out at last when the women entice her with their dancing. When I do Tai Chi out on the knoll in the Summer months I often face the sun and tell Amaterasu I come dancing for her, not to entice her but to thank her for her gifts. Year 'round I bathe in liquid sunlight in my clawfoot tub, and read by sunlight transformed and emanating from glass orbs. In the cold of Winter I am warmed by the sun's energy contained in the bodies of trees. My table bears the nourishing fruits of photosynthesis.

And when my work here on this cellar is complete, there will be shelves to hold, among other things, apples and canned vegetables from our sunny garden. The sun provides them all, with not a little help, of course, from earth and air and water. This Winter when I come searching for some ingredients for a hearty soup, or filling for my staple pies, Amaterasu will peek out from a cellar of her own and light my way among the shelves.

Friday, November 4

It has been raining steadily since I awoke this early morning and it shows no sign of letting up as the afternoon passes. I had planned to finish the door today, but the rain has taken my workspace on the deck, the only outdoor flat space available. So I am having a somewhat lazy day, with minor accomplishments. A little frustrating. The unstructured time was even rather awkward at first, which tells me it is a good thing to be reminded of the value of a leisurely day now and again.

When I returned to work yesterday morning after five days of other commitments, the weather had changed drastically. It was as though I had left in one season and returned in another. The temperature had dropped 20° since last week's 50s when I put away my tools. Now yet an additional shirt layer was required, as well as long underwear under my sweatpants. I soon discovered my thin cotton gloves were inadequate against the biting cold, so I dug out the polypropylene liners from the bottom of the glove box. Then I was cozy enough, so long as I kept working. In this manner I finished the last of the walls and did the final installation of the light switch with its cover. Looks real professional, I must say.

The time has changed in the last week too, fallen back an hour, so the darkness comes much earlier in the afternoon, the hours available for work getting shorter as the planet flies from the sun. After lunch yesterday, before returning to the cellar, I brought the extension ladder from where it hangs on the side of the house facing the forest and placed it against the eave for access to the roof. I took a couple of wrenches and a hammer and went up to adjust the solar electricity panels to place them more directly in the line of the Winter sun's rays. It was an easy job, and I enjoyed the opportunity to be on the roof, now that the thick morning frost had melted. From up there I can see the whole amphitheater of the garden which occupies the slope down from the house, and more of the ridges stretching out to the south. Much of the garden begins to turn from Summer's green to Autumn's browns and eventually we will complete the browning with the Winter mulch of leaves. But there are patches of bright green in a few beds where we have sown crimson clover to be a nitrogen-giving cover crop. They look like brand new blankets tucked carefully into place.

Then, in the afternoon, before the darkness came, I managed to get most of the boards cut for the door and assembled the outer frame. I braced it on the diagonal with a thin board and temporarily set it in place to test the fit. I've always said lumber is living, breathing material with a mind of its own, so I was not surprised that the fit was too snug even though a double check of all the measurements showed no mistake. I left the frame in place in the opening and quit for the day, glad for the warmth of the house and the hot dinner I'd make.

Today's cold wet weather has kept me in the house, and grateful for the well-seasoned firewood stacked neatly beneath the new woodshed roof. One thing I did accomplish while it rained was to paint the three large T-strap hinges, bolt slide, door-pull, and screw heads for the door, all a jet black. I already had all these things, except the screws, picked up here and there or left over from prior projects. The slide bolt and door-pull required some work with knife and sandpaper to remove chips of old paint and rust. The pull was something I salvaged when we tore down the old outhouse years ago, after I had built the fine composting privy. I sanded away history and painted on a shiny promise of an old function for a new door.

Saturday, November 6

Hanging that door turned out to be a major project in itself. Because I wanted to be able to install it without having to ask, or wait, for help from someone else, I kept its weight at the minimum by attaching only the outside sheet of plywood to the $2'' \times 4''$ frame. Then I could lift it in and out of the door opening in the front wall by myself. Not that it was a light load, but it was manageable. Thank goodness I had thought to proceed this way, because I lost count of how many times I lifted the door into place and screwed down the three big hinges onto the door jamb, only to have to take it out again to work yet more on the fit. I must have repeated this maneuver a dozen times and planed an eighth of an inch off the closing edge, before the door finally was willing to close into the recess. I wanted a good fit, wanted the door to snug up tight against the weatherstripping taped along the edges of the door stops, wooden strips I'd nailed onto the jambs. I wanted to prevent any access for even the smallest insects, like the little moths who might come seeking the relative warmth of the cellar and prowl for sustenance among the contents of cardboard boxes.

Working with hand tools gives me a sense of myself as a traditional artisan, and this is especially true when I use the planes. I suppose the finer details of plane design have changed over time, but these tools feel in my hands like close sisters to those used for centuries in the woodshops of the Old World and the New. As I am pushing the body of the plane along the wood, directing the sharp blade to its work, I conjure a kinship with women in long skirts and bandanas who may have stolen into a male relative's domain and secretly made the curls of wood emerge as they planed a scrap. Or maybe there were women whose yearning for the trade bade them dress in men's clothing, crop their hair, and bind their bosoms so they could pass into the world of the guilds and apprenticeships. In these or some other guises, I imagine women like myself bending with the tool and satisfying some deep aesthetic hunger.

Guided by only the light of the day, my cellar door propped securely against the well-worn sawhorses, I used three different planes as required by the turn of the wood or the thickness of the shaving I wanted to remove, or how close to the end of the board I was getting, or just according to the appropriateness of the various planes, which does change with the ambient temperature, the density of the lumber, and their individual moods and personalities. I have found that a given plane, like the nine-inch smoothing plane I bought at a second-hand store, and cleaned and restored to good use, will work splendidly with one project but refuse to function well with another. And the multi-talented, fifteen-inch, hand-crafted rose-wood jack plane, itself a work of art, will deftly chase a warped irregularity from a surface with just a few passes, or coax a hair's thickness from a near-fit. The shorter, block planes took off any roughness left by the handsaw on the ends of the boards.

I hardly felt the cold damp November air as I passed the planes again and again along the edge, working to a sweat as I breathed in rhythm with the song of the tool in my hand. When finally I was satisfied with the fit, I secured the screws in the hinges and proceeded to staple on the insulation, then affixed the inside panel of plywood I had already cut. Alas, with that addition the door changed shape! Apparently the inner panel compromised with the outer panel and together they pulled the frame to their liking, and the door I had labored on so long would no longer close. So off it came again, more planing and testing, and eventually I had a hanging, opening-and-closing, snug-fitting door. I, and my forebears, were very proud, both of the door and of my perseverance through the day.

Monday, November 8

I started work early today, since I have just three more days remaining in the time I have scheduled to complete this project, before other work, commitments, and plans will edge it aside. Because the temperature has remained consistently below the required minimum of 50°, I probably will not be able to apply the solid color stain to three of the walls until next Spring, so that finishing touch will wait. I'll look forward to the effect the color "Stonehedge" will have on the old plywood. I plan to use the cedar shakes left from the exterior of the house for the door and front wall, though this too may have to wait until Spring, unless a couple of warmish Winter days stir me to carpentry. For now, I want to complete the two banks of shelves and cover the front wall and door with black roofing felt.

Yesterday I started to carry up from the old barn the 2″ × 12″ boards I'll use for some of the shelving. Each one is heavy, just over five feet long, and the path between the barn and my house is one of the steeper ones on this hillside homestead, so the going was slow and I was panting mightily by the time I reached the cellar. I figure to bring the eight of them up in stages, two today, two or maybe four more tomorrow, the rest the next day, by when I plan to have the shelf frames ready for them. A lot of the shelving is made from the extra sheets of the reject plywood, starting with the pieces left from the cutting of the wall panels.

This part of the construction has me working inside the cellar a lot, measuring and installing the $2'' \times 4''$ frame members that I saw to length outside. The difference in humidity between the two is very apparent as I step from one to the other and close the door behind me. The temperature difference is not all that great, 44° inside to a 40° outside, but the good job I did with insulation and caulk makes the inside so dry it feels lots warmer, and I have to remove my hat to let out some body heat when I work in there. I designed the shelves to use as little $2'' \times 4''$ lumber as possible, because the stock gleaned from the water tank is getting very low. Today I completed the east bank, making the spaces just right for fitting in crates of apples under the bottom shelf, and rows of canned goods to fill the others, with a high space between the top shelf and the underbelly of the house for boxes. With one wall covered now with shelves, the purpose behind all this work becomes manifest.

Wednesday, November 10

Yesterday I skipped a day on the cellar to keep a promise to Bethroot that I would do some work with her in her new house. There are doors to hang there too! For over a year the two little odd-shaped and extremely heavy doors, which will eventually give access to a woodbin, have just sat in place in their openings, allowing the cold Winter air to sneak in around them. One Winter with blankets hanging strategically over them was enough for Bethroot, so I agreed to what we thought would be an easy afternoon's work. After my experience with the cellar door only a few days ago, I should have known better! We hung the bigger of the two, a trapezoid five feet on its longest side, but then it refused to open until I had incrementally sawed off and planed a wide segment of the edge. We managed to get it successfully and permanently installed just as there would have been too little daylight to be able to work on it any further. I was grateful for the hot meal Bethroot rewarded us with, and glad to share the apple pie I'd made that morning.

While the pie had baked I labored up three more of those $2'' \times 12''$ boards from the barn, getting that task more than half-way done. Then, first thing this morning, I went down and got the remaining three, taking it slowly, stopping often to breathe as I trudged up the hill. Muphin provided a sniffing companionship as she scouted wild scents along the way. Perhaps she got a whiff of whoever is marauding the buckets of apples waiting on the trailer porch and destined for the new cellar. I figure it's a raccoon, or maybe more than one, and I'll be glad when I can get the fruit out of their reach.

The remaining shelves went up easily today, everything fitting just right. The space of the cellar is not all that big, just over 50 square feet, so when I got the frame built for the west bank of shelves the cellar began to feel a bit like a walk-in closet. I worried about this a little while, wondering if I was making it too difficult to maneuver boxes into place, but then decided that I would be able to manage all right.

Whereas I had to make several cuts on the plywood sheets to get the pieces needed for each shelf, the old barn boards required just one angled cross-cut and they dropped easily into place. These boards were once the surface of a long ramp extending from the ground up to the second story of the barn, said by the realtor when we bought the place to be about sixty years old. I intend to bear sixty years (in just five more) much better than this barn has. The roof has a sway-back suggestive of an aged trailhorse, and has lost from the furring strips large patches of its hand-hewn wooden shingles. The foundation rested on huge cedar rounds which commenced to rot out from under the posts, until Bethroot organized a work party to replace them with concrete piers five years ago. The pole rafters, no doubt cut from the surrounding forest, were pulling away from the beams so badly that in some cases it was the roof holding up the rafter rather than the other way around. So Bethroot researched what to do about the problem and rented equipment to band the rafter ends and beams together, so no further separation would be possible. At the time, I would have let the old barn fall down and salvage what materials we could from it for other projects on the land, but Bethroot, who has a reverence for history, saw the beauty in the old structure and wanted to preserve it. A dozen or so women came to help, some working from scaffolds to do the banding, others pulling the roof closer to its original shape with come-alongs, still others wrestling with the piers and jacks. One woman made the much-appreciated contribution of a hot lunch for all of us. And so the barn still stands, bearing the weight of her years of use with more security. Visiting women often choose to sleep under its light-dotted roof and gaze through the holes into the starry sky, listening to the night sounds.

The foundation for the long ramp had rotted, so it was shortened and a ladder added for access to the upper floor. Thus there were ramp boards left over and the sixteen of them were neatly stacked out of the weather to await some future use. Since then Bethroot has built this new house for herself, taking these three years to work with a dyke carpenter/forewoman and a total of close to seventy periodic helpers, most of them volunteers, to create a beautiful ten-sided house further up the hill. With this building has come for us the hope of greater harmony as we continue to share the loving and tending of the land, and the hosting of our gatherings. We divided that stack of boards in half, my share to become shelving, hers yet to be assigned their new life. As I worked with my eight yesterday, I studied the raised grain of the grey wood long-exposed to the weather, and fantasized about the animals and people who used the ramp when the barn was built over a half-century ago by the Pate family, the original homesteaders.

One Autumn day shortly after we moved here in '76, two middle-aged women and one of their daughters walked the whole way up our road to pay a call. They introduced themselves as Pates by their maiden names, said they had lived here as children.

They hadn't lived in this area of the county in a long while and hadn't been back to see their childhood home. Bethroot and I were delighted to meet them and walk briefly around the land with them, hearing stories of their family life here in the '30s and '40s. Turns out one of their homesteading parents was originally from Tennessee – as is Bethroot – the other from Pennsylvania – as am I. These women came here to touch something precious from their past and without knowing it gave my land partner and me a boost into the future, as though they had gently held us in their hands and released us for our flight. I don't know why the Pates left this land, what adversity may have driven them to towns, dispersed their family. It is as though the land called Bethroot and me to her, to take up where the others left off, to continue this northern-southern alliance.

There are initials carved into one of the old posts of the west barn wall, M.P. + S.K. Maybe one of our Pate visitors recorded there a secret loving that remains sealed in the wood, a loving Bethroot and I and our community have honored with our preserving labor, and the fullness of our Lesbian lives.

Musing thusly, the cold and rain of this last day of construction did not bother me so much, and I had the shelves completed by late afternoon, as well as shallow pallets on the floor to hold the crates of apples. There remained only to attach the roofing paper to the door and front wall, as well as clean up the entire working area, sort and stack the leftover plywood and lumber, and put away the array of tools and supplies this project has called from my workbench area in the house. My satisfaction was deep and warm as I stood admiring my accomplishment, the outside dimly lit by the waning day, the inside bathed with transformed sunlight at a mere flip of a switch. Then into the house for supper and a deep hot bath, the water for which had been heated all day by the thermosiphon loop through the woodstove. I soaked the chill out of my exhaustion, and went to bed with a smiling pride.

Arborescent

This has been a fine day. The sun came back for at least a visit after so many many days of cloudy, rainy skies. I labored mightily yesterday to extensively improve the drainage ditch along the road, in case last week's torrent repeats itself. This morning I had a few sore muscles, which gave me permission for lighter work and a leisurely walk. I completed several small tasks, then set out with my camera and Muphin's bounding enthusiasm. I have been wanting to photograph some particular trees, so today's clear weather was my first opportunity and I thought I had better make use of it.

First down to the old barn. In November there was a big snow storm here, with a foot of snow on the ground and heavy on the trees. The unusual weight brought down one of the six locusts in the barnyard, as well as large parts of the lilac bushes on the knoll, and a few small firs and madrones on the path to the Poogoda. I've cut up the trees on the path, but have yet to get to the lilacs, or this locust. It is a heavy hardwood, its length just missing by inches the east barn wall when it fell.

When I first visited the barn after the snow had melted, I was impressed by the fact that this tree had actually been two trees in one. There had been two separate trunks growing from a single base; when the tree fell, the trunks toppled in opposite directions, each falling back from the center. Although surely the snow must have been a serious catalyst in the breaking asunder, I think it was actually just the last straw in a demise which had been approaching for some time. As I closely inspected the stump, where the two had been joined together, I found there was rot in the wood. Strange. There had been the usual abundance of clusters of sweet-smelling white flowers last Spring, and no suggestion of decay I took notice of then. Nonetheless, there was death in the tree, brewing undetected even while she bloomed.

I photographed from several angles, trying to record something of the drama of the scene. As I studied the locust, I thought about the falling apart that happened to my mate and me eleven years ago. I have often held that time as a failure, another case of a Lesbian relationship not "making it." She moved back to the city, we split up, and I eventually resolutely chose my singleness. I have worked hard in these years to understand the mistakes I made, the malignant patterns I enacted or participated in. This has been important work and I am healthier for it. At the same time, the locust gives me a different perspective on the subject. I am cautioned to remember there is more to the story of this tree than its disease, its fatal weakness. For more than twenty years it had stood in the barnyard and, along with its sisters, filled the air each Spring with a fragrance worth the walk down, and back up, the hill. Now I stroked the wet rough bark and my hands easily remembered the loving my mate and I made together, the mostly good and vibrant life we shared for over five years. But just as those two trunks could stand for only so long on what gave them their beginning, my love and I could stay together only so long as what we were creating was good for both of us, and that had come to an end. The sadness is that so much suffering attended our leave-taking. Like the dyad lying in the barnyard, we each had our own experience of a toppling, deprived of the foundation we had come to depend upon.

It will take a lot of energy, my ditch-digging muscles recovered and ready for the job, to cut the locust to manageable lengths and haul them out of the way. The tree, and the work, will wait.

After my musing at the barn, Muphin and I hiked up the hill to visit again the madrones I discovered a week or so ago, when a break in the heavy rain gave both of us some desperately needed fresh air and physical exercise. There is a path which goes off into the forest about halfway up to the north boundary of these forty acres, an old logging track bearing lots of young firs, making it difficult to get through in places, though short-legged Muphin had no trouble. On that prior walk I had spied a strange-looking configuration of trees up the bank from the path and climbed up the slippery clay slope to investigate. Today I easily found again the two small madrones, each about eight inches in diameter, who had apparently been forced into an amazing intimacy some years back. One of them had grown to lie across the other; their trunks were overlapping about seven feet up from the ground. And not just overlapping, like one hand embraced in the palm of another. These two trees had taken each other on at cellular level: the bark of one comingled with that of the other, the two trees sharing one bark covering where they crossed. I climbed a nearby madrone to get a better look, trying to find a flaw in this apparent merger, some incomplete place on the unitrunk. But their blending was perfect. At the place where the two trees held each other, they had become one tree. But only at that place. They each had a history before their melding, and they each continued on singly, and in different directions, from their union.

I found a thick tuft of bear grass in a small patch of noontime sun where I could sit and think, while Muphin nosed about in the forest nearby.

Had my mate and I come that close, so enmeshed with each other? I know that depth of merger, of sharing one life, is what I wanted. That is what I thought true love was supposed to be about, the ultimate goal possible for, and only in, Lesbian loving. But I have known one of my jobs is to change the way I have been prone to love, to let go of this desire to merge with my lover.

I do see the necessity for this change: in all my attempts at mergers in my loving I have always turned my back on myself, stunting my own growth, sacrificing too much of my identity in the name of commitment. Perhaps in this I have sought to return to the prenatal being of the same body as my mother. And there is that other mother, the Earth, from whose matter I am made and into whose womb I shall indeed return. Being-at-one-with is my beginning and ending in this life, an instinct for bonding that speaks to the original and final reality of my physical existence. But I see this instinct has not served me well for the decades in between.

The sun had shifted, a wind had risen as the afternoon gained; I sat now in shade too cool for comfort. I went back to the madrones, reached up and caressed their bonding with admitted envy. I noted the small side branches and vibrant green leaves each of them had birthed as they grew on and away from each other. Each came to their mating with their individuality and left with it intact. I looked with imagination's eye beneath their shared bark and saw the wood of each that had not stopped growing. It had been possible for these two madrones to encase themselves in a shared identity for a passionate pass of time, and then part with no apparent sacrifice.

We continued from there up to the small clearing which marks the northern boundary, where I wanted to complete this photo-graphic study. One of the first things I discovered as I began walking this land, in 1976, was the assault recently made on the madrones in the government-owned forest bordering this property on the north. A killing girdle had been chainsawed around the trunk of each madrone, deep into the cambium layer, severing the fibers that carry the nutrients for sustenance and growth. This guaranteed a slow and certain death, freeing soil, water and light for the benefit of the adjacent firs and cedars, the so-called marketable timber. The forest up there is pocked with the steady demise of grand madrones. I have watched these nearly twenty years as their massive trunks have slowly metamorphosed from beige/green/orange/gold ochre to black, then bleaching out to grey. Watched the leaves wither and fall, not to be replaced, the smaller branches break off, leaving pale standing skeletons, denuded of the flaky bark.

In the early years of this vigil, when the drama of the madrones presented a slightly different scene each time I visited them, I observed one tree whose large southernmost top fork still held bright green leaves, the golden ochre trunk reaching like a woman's glistening flexed muscle into the sky above the conifers. Curious, I pushed through thick poison oak and wild honeysuckle vines, tripped over rotting logs on the forest floor, to stand beside this apparent survivor of the loggers' sweep. There I found what seemed to me a miracle: the ugly gash around the bark was there, but on the southern side of the tree, the side that faces the nearby clearing where I had been singing my mourning and praising songs, this tree had knit herself back together over a small section of the wound. Curly reddish-brown bark flecked on green-ochre new growth, which flowed like hardened liquid over the cut, making a life-sustaining bridge about eight inches wide. I could almost feel the fluids of the tree pulsing through her brave viaduct.

This survivor has been an inspiring companion for me these many years, especially when I have felt my own lust for life become frail from heart-breaking disappointment, when it seemed a wound had gone too deep for healing. This living tree whose name I share makes mockery of my despair, and I too find a passageway to my roots, and keep on growing. Life did not end with the slicing my mate and I had to do, though it sometimes felt to me like it would. In truth, we have each mended ourselves, are glistening and strong, doing the loving and the good work we are each given to do in our parted lives.

Today, holding my camera safely against my chest, I trudged through the thick brush and celebrated this forest familiar with her portrait.

On the walk back down the hill I was charmed by a little yellow violet growing in the path, then two stumps, one lavishly covered with horseshoe lichens, the other boasting a cluster of fairy cups laden with seed coinage. The sky announced the bright sunshine's visit finished for now, with the return of this season's near-constant fare, beginning with a sprinkle, then turning to a downpour by the time we reached the house. I built up the fire in the stove, then Muphin and I sat in front of its opened double doors, warmed and dried by the burning logs while the rain pounded on the roof. I rested easily, knowing the good work I had done on the ditch, knowing the good work I have done.

Altaring

Last mid-Winter a letter came from Kay Turner, a Lesbian who was gathering material for a book about women and their altars, asking if she could visit and interview my land partner and me in early Spring. Bethroot would be away on a trip then, but I welcomed the visit, intrigued by the topic which rested in the back of my mind as I went about the seasonal work of the land.

When we built a new wire fence around the garden in the early 1980s we squared out the fence line from its former irregular shape and enclosed about six hundred square feet, a much larger area than the old collapsing fence had corralled. Since then two large blackberry/fern patches as well as expanded vegetable and flower beds have enjoyed fool-proof (well, almost) protection from the deer, raccoons, and our small flock of hens. The wild vines claim a ten foot wide swath all along the bottom fence line and, near the top line, have taken over about a fifth of the total garden area. I have studied that upper bramble these many years and wished I had the time and perseverance to clear it all away and plant an orchard, to add variety to our harvest from the apple trees in the old orchard down the draw, below the garden. We have tried to introduce other fruits down there: a nectarine one year, a sour cherry another. But they both died, one from disease and the other from the nibbling of the deer who persisted through every barrier we erected. We gave up the thought of populating the orchard with other fruit, and I have long had my eye on that fenced-in blackberry patch at the top of the garden.

Because the garden is terraced on a hill, the watering of the vegetable beds eventually feeds the lower berry patch, and each year I am grateful for the fat berries I pick fresh for breakfasts and pies, and the several batches I preserve. But the upper patch gets only the water from a rainfall, and Summers here have tended to be very dry, so there is a paucity of berries in a lot of space. But too much space to tackle for eradicating all those blackberry vines and ferns, or so I've always concluded when I have imagined the task.

Early last November a friend in town gave me several persimmons from her backyard tree she had planted four years before. I'd never eaten a persimmon before, and discovered I love the fruit. This was a variety, the Fuyu, not astringent, as apparently many persimmons are; not extremely sweet, but smooth and sweet enough. My seduced palate prompted me to reconsider that bramble in the garden. Instead of envisioning the whole patch cleared out, which would take weeks of grunt work, why not clear a space big enough for just one tree?! I located a nursery about an hour from home where the Fuyu was stocked, and set to work one warm February day.

The canes lay in layer upon layer, the oldest spent canes lying nearest the earth where they were moist and rotting. Above that layer were brown, brittle stalks, most of which ran in a tangled confusion for many feet. And yet above those was an equally knotted mass of younger growth, the canes arcing over and under each other. With long-handled loppers I cut into this labyrinth, piled what I was able to pull free, and hauled those piles with a spading fork out of the garden to a space beneath some trees where they will metamorphose into earth. Little by little I worked to within sight of the soil laced with many years' accumulation of composted vines and fern fronds. Then I thought I'd dig out the roots, to remove any possibility of reappearance. But once I got started with the shovel I soon learned the prospect of eliminating the roots to their foot, or greater, depth would be a gargantuan task, for the soil was run through with roots of various generations, from the pencil-thin new shoots to the aged gnarled thick snakes, which must have begun their meanderings decades before I fantasized a tame orchard in the place of the wild patch. I decided to leave the soil relatively undisturbed, except for where I'd plant the tree, and just keep the area mowed. I have done this in other sections of the garden, and over time the vines no longer come up, the roots decay from lack of feeding from leaves, thereby adding their bodies to the richness of the soil, and grass eventually covers the exposure.

It was a late March day when I brought the persimmon home, its tender roots in a plastic bag, the whole six-foot length of the young tree just barely fitting in a stretch from the back seat of my car to the front window. Though the weather was still cold and wet, and sometimes snowy, the nurserywoman encouraged me to get the bare-root tree into the ground. The next day, when there was a sunny hiatus, I dug with the strong old metal-handled shovel into a threaded maze of blackberry and fern roots. The going was slow and arduous as I wrested one root after another from the rain-loosened soil in a four-foot square space. Now and again I stopped, leaned on the shovel and thankfully breathed in the warm air. Sunshine glowed all around me, pulling steam from the sodden earth, a magical interplay of earth and fire, water and air.

I mixed in a sack of compost, then removed the soil-compost mix to about a foot's depth. Up on the lane I loaded two bags of leaves into a wheelbarrow, then gently removed the persimmon from my car and laid it on top of the bags. It was a little awkward getting all of that down the hill and through the gateway between the tall cedar and fir, standing like Doric columns at the northern entrance to the garden, our vegetable-growing temple.

I set the sapling, sporting a dozen or so branch-promising buds, into the hole, and coaxed the roots to spread and settle in the soil. Then I pulled in most of what I had spaded out, packing soil firmly around the roots and the short length of the stem below the surface. I watered it well, then added the rest of the soil and dumped leaves all around the base of the tree, making a four-foot diameter circle of mulch, about eight inches deep.

The nurserywoman had instructed me to snip off the top few inches, which would begin the pattern I'll want of widening more than heightening. I explained this to the persimmon as I did the pruning, then caressed her long thumb-thick body and sang a welcome to this land, to my life. I kissed the grey skin of the young tree several times up and down her length, lightly touched the buds, encouraging her acclimation, reaching through her dormancy to her strong spirit.

For the next couple of days there were snow flurries and temperatures around freezing; it felt more like Winter than much of January had. I worried about how the new tree was doing, frequently stood at a window to gaze down the hill at her, and visited her several times to offer gentle reassurances. The top I had pruned stood in a short vase on the kitchen windowsill where I could watch the buds swell and green. Then the next week the weather turned sunny again and I got the kale, Pak Choi, chard, mustard and spinach sowed on a day when it was warm enough to roll up my shirtsleeves.

The planting was experimental this year, inspired by a friend's report from a permaculture gardening workshop she attended. Listening to her, I realized that all these years I have unconsciously related to the soil as merely a receptacle for seed, a receptacle which requires my tilling and addition of fertilizer – dependent upon my hard work in order to be an effective host for the seeds and plants I place there. But the workshop teacher described the soil in more womanly terms as a living organism, a being to be respected and not unduly disturbed, who is willing to include my desires in her grand scheme of self-nurturance. The soil is rich with her own life processes, and hosts insects and animals who work with her to create an environment already perfect for growing plants. What *is* important for me to add is mulch: I must do the task the deciduous trees would do if I let them grow in my garden, where they would naturally drop their yearly treasure that controls erosion, makes a healthy environment for the earthworms, and eventually breaks down to become soil again.

As I planted the seeds for the greens, it was easy to feel in the company of another being. Kneeling beside the bed, I disturbed her as little as possible after I pulled aside the Winter covering of leaves to outline the rows. I tickled the top inch or so of the dark soil with my trowel, dropped the seeds into the small loose irregularities, and then patted the soil over the seeds, a planting task that became an intimate exercise.

It was easy to feel in other company as well, as I imagined Lesbians in their gardens up and down the interstate and across the country, around the planet. I wondered where else my people were sowing seed, or would plant a fruit tree this year. Though I cherish my solitude, and love to work in the garden alone, I am happily aware of the wide circle of gardening/planting women. As the sun warmed my back and my hands patted the cool earth, I chanted a blessing to the seeds, asked for their abundant germination, and keenly felt the presence of this circle.

The weather continued in a seesaw fashion, and I followed suit by reading, knitting, and doing some small repairs at my workbench on the cold wet days, and working in my flower garden near the house when the sky cleared for a few hours now and again. I carefully pinched back the infant mums, weeded among the lupines, thinned the congested love-in-a-mist seedlings coming up in the Wildbed. The last of the big daffodils and the first of the red and yellow tulips cheerfully greeted me as I made my way among the beds. The hydrangeas were bright with new foliage, the climbing rose on the henhouse full of tiny promises of bloom. I lamented that the late severe frosts had killed most of the hundreds of flower buds on the wisteria; the sweet purple show would be much diminished this year. As I pulled some sorrel from the base of the pink-flowering azalea, the ambrosial scent of the nearby daphne made me stop, stand tall, and breathe long and deep.

It was good, then, to pause in my puttering and sit for a spell on the cedar bench I built over ten years ago at my dogfriend

Phyrste's grave, where the Michaelmas daisies were just beginning to come up. I discovered the rose planted there among the daisies had a crippled stem, no doubt from a snowfall heavier than it was prepared to carry. I got a stick and some tape from the house and made a splint to hold the stem upright so it could mend. Over to the left of Phyrste's grave, Little Lavy lies buried beneath a Lavender plant, and Ladydog in the dahlia bed. Missy Moonshine's grave had been marked with a large cross-section of madrone, and Black-Eyed Susans to honor her calico colors. Caius' heather has spread wide since I transplanted it here nearly nineteen years ago, brought from the big Shepherd's grave over at the coast. I was surrounded by reminders of my animal friends, yet another of the circles in which I live.

On one of the last sunny days we were to have for several weeks, Kay, the woman authoring the book about altars, came for our prearranged interview. She arrived as I was having lunch, so she joined me for a sandwich and some easy getting-acquainted. Eventually we took off our shoes and went into the inner circle of my round house, into the twelve-foot diameter space enclosed by the posts which hold up the roof and the central loft. We settled ourselves on the rug and I talked about the specific items on my altar, about what I do with them each day, and about how my altar differs from both the concept and the reality of the altar of the church in my childhood. That Lutheran altar had a sense of taboo about it; it was untouchable by the likes of me, or apparently by everyone but the minister. And it was set up above the congregation, higher than us, apart from us, presumably because the worshipped was higher than the worshippers, as though that separation made for the mystery and power of the altar.

How different is the altar in my home: a round piece of plywood covered by a large doily made by Bethroot's great aunt, and objects I am intimate with: rocks and crystals, locks of hair from each of the animal companions buried in the flower garden, a rattle made from a stick and large round seed pods – given to me by a dear friend – a bundle of sage from eastern Oregon, a pebble left a few years ago by my mother with whom I have a sometimes strained relationship, an ornament of beadwork made by my grandmother, some pieces of madrone bark . . . all things I frequently hold while I meditate. I don't relate to these "sacred" objects in a hocus-pocus way, don't imbue them with a magic any greater, or less, than the magic of the seasons, of growth, death, and return. My altar is a microcosm of myself, of my living, and not a static assemblage of things. As I spoke all this, it dawned on me that *altar* is not only a noun but also a verb. "To altar." I altar, which is to say I focus, concentrate on whatever is up (an illness, someone I want to sing heartfullness to, something I am grateful for); I give myself healing touch, speak my list of affirmations. Sometimes I do emotional release if I have the need, and a polished rock, a slice of petrified wood, an old wooden candlestick conjure the company of women who care about me. And whatever I do, I am always in communion with the circle of women who gather within these posts every quarter holiday, when this altar is the center for our altaring.

After my visitor left I ambled among the flower beds, sang a cheering hello to the persimmon, spoke encouragement to the vegetable seeds swelling in their wet berths, and thought more about my spiritual practise in its country Lesbian context. I understood that the altaring I do daily in the inner circle of the house is similar to what I do with plants and soil: it feels the same to focus on the candle flame as to contemplate the earth's moisture rising to the sun, the same to hold a crystal and call healing to a friend as to splint a rose branch. I meditate on rooting out the enmity in my life, and I pull roots from their moorings. I touch a pressure point on my body, and I pat soil over seeds, wrap my fingers around the new young tree. I affirm my becoming who I want to be, and I transform a bramble into an orchard.

Winter persisted into April. I got the pots seeded for the coldframe on the deck but did little further outdoor work. I continued to muse about altars and altaring until one day, after watering the coldframe, I stood a long while on the deck and considered the gardens, the old lower orchard, the snow lingering on the distant ridges, the huge white clouds, and understood the immensity, the mystery and power, of the altar that is the Earth herself. On this altar I am an active sacred object. In the myriad details of my daily living, I manifest the goddess speaking her affirmations. Whether my heart sings in the area enclosed by rafter-holding posts, or the garden fence, or the ridge-caressing sky, or the expanding boundaries of my philosophy, I am held and defined by concentric circles of altaring.

Daring Acquiescence

There is rarely a lack of challenges in this Lesbian life, this country Lesbian life. Sometimes they are on the mundane side, like getting some vegetable or another to succeed in a garden bed that year after year hosts a failure, or figuring out how to make the flow from the mountain spring enter the spring tank, despite the defiance of leaves, tiny stones and twigs, wanting to block its way. More dramatically, when the Autumn rains pummel this hillside for days at a time, it takes an amateur's degree in hydrodynamics to tame the run-off which eats at the side of the ditch along our road.

Over these nearly two decades I have enjoyed the challenges inherent in country living, and have steadily invented and added ones of my own to what the land provides. With little developed skill but with great intention, I determined to carpenter an unfinished skeleton of a house into a beautiful and comfortable home, metamorphose a clay patch into a green lawn, a blackberry bramble into the beginnings of an orchard. The challenges, and the work they require, keep me busy, keep me learning, keep me accomplishing.

Maybe it's some seasonal spiralling in myself that has me taking a look, just a little peek, mind you, at letting go of a challenge here and there, letting one pass me by once in a very great while. In fact, this year I made a conscious decision to let the weeds grow in the thirty feet of gravel path leading from the gate, in the deer-and-chicken-proof fence, to my house. I wanted to eliminate the constant challenge of pulling up the creeping clover, lawn daisies, moss, and occasional sprigs of grass, or the periodic arduous job of spending hours on my knees taking them out with a clawed cultivator. I decided to give up the image of a pristine path of stones I have labored to maintain these many years. But I felt some defeat in this, some disappointment in myself, some worry about letting things slip. What would be next?

This is tricky business. I keep a strict watchful eye on myself, being careful to discern between healthfully-shifting priorities, and a lazy backsliding into what is only adequate, and thus less than what would most cultivate and spur me to new growth.

Last Winter I wanted to visit the biggest surviving madrone tree far up in the government-owned forest beyond our northern boundary, to walk where the snow was virgin, except for whatever wild creatures had left their tracks. And indeed they had! On our way up the hill Muphin sniffed out the usual signs of deer, with their forked hoofprints, a few rabbit tracks, and possibly the signature of a big bird dragging her long tail between snow-piercing hops. I added my tracks to theirs as I trudged through the ankle-deep snow.

Soon after I left the open path just above our property line, I entered the thick forest on an old logging track. About fifty feet down from that juncture I came upon a serious obstacle: several huge madrones had fallen alongside, and over, the path. They had pulled with them a few large firs, knocked down many young conifers and deciduous bushes, bent over others still holding onto life, though with a twisted future in store.

I could not see how I'd get through that snow-covered maze, and announced to Muphin I was turning back. I thought I'd return in the Spring, perhaps with an axe and a saw, and make a more facile access through the labyrinth of massive trunks and branches. But as I retraced a few steps I realized this was a new experience for me on this land: I was giving up a goal because of some physical challenge, giving in to a want for ease. That did not set well in me: it felt too soon, and I too young, in my mid-fifties, to retreat from obstacles, to come away from an intent for a forest walk in so quick a defeat. So I turned around and followed a happy Muphin into the thicket. While she sprinted easily from trunk to trunk like a circus acrobat, I laboriously made my way, sometimes straddling, sometimes bending beneath the tangle, crawling on all fours in the snow where the only passage was under a mammoth wooden torso, stretched like a low lintel across the path. A thin branch whipped my cheek as I stumbled my way through the drama of fallen trees. I was duly pleased with myself when I reached the other side, where I could stand and walk with relative ease again.

It was good to visit the big live madrone, to see the last rays of the Winter sun kiss her glowing amber bark. She rises like a grand monument there among the firs, always ready to remind me of strength and purpose, of challenges best met head-on, and not avoided.

Still, there are other double-dares sent my way, when what is wanted is not a heroic perseverance, but the grace of stepping aside.

A few years ago Bethroot and I had just settled quietly to an evening snack when we heard Moongoose suddenly squawking in apparent terror. She always roosted on a large rock outside the nearby henhouse, and it sounded like she might be trying to fend off disaster. Bethroot ran to grab a flashlight, while I, thinking I'd catch a raccoon or some such predator in the act of attacking the big grey goose, dashed out the back door and down the steps. I was yelling: "Hey! Scat!!" as I neared the corner of the henhouse, Bethroot by then shouting her own version of scare tactics from the top of the steps and waving a beam on the scene. Just as I got close to the door, I saw this was no raccoon to whom I was confidently blaring orders. Stretched out at least a good eight feet on the ground, with the goose's bones audibly snapping in her jaws, was a mountain lion, her tawny coat almost blending with the twilight. In little more time than it takes to say "Oh . . . Puma," I stopped, turned into Bethroot's light, and was back up the steps and into the house. There was no sense of defeat in my retreat: I was no match for the hungry big cat making her uncontestable claim on our friend.

When to persevere, and when to yield? When to hold on to an intention, and when to let it go? Honing a wisdom about this dilemma is a challenge in itself.

Early last Summer my former mate wrote to me, in gentle and loving terms, about the Lesbian wedding she and her partner were planning for September, in the city where they live several hours from here. She so much hoped I would come. My steadfast love for her, and my wishing her and her new mate a happy life, spurred me to want to attend; my fear of being overwhelmed by the scene, and having old pain restimulated, cautioned me to stay home. In the successive weeks I did Tai Chi with this question, now pushing myself forward to a magnanimous gesture, now pulling back and letting the event pass me by. When the printed invitation arrived, with its details about the ceremony, reception and dance, my retreat was tangible. I asked myself again and again if my reluctance was like the fallen trees on the logging track, an obstacle to be acknowledged but overcome, with a promise of beauty beyond? Or was I face-to-face with a lion-sized deterrent to a heroic deed, one to be honored and made peace with? I worried I would be forever disappointed in myself if I did not strain at my limits, but in the end I listened to my growing desire to not have to work so hard, to not have to accept every challenge my life offers. The weeds growing among the gravel helped me with this decision: the regular watering of the lawn had encouraged them to spread, and I began to see that the greening path did not look all that bad after all, just different, possibly even attractive.

With Bethroot as carrier, I sent a vase of flowers from my garden to the wedding, and on the day of the grand event I sat before my altar and asked myself to meditate on whatever blessing I could fully and truthfully intend. Instead of any dissatisfaction with my choice to stay home, or feeling less than the goddess I aspire to be, I swelled with abundant love: for the wedding women, and for myself.

Perhaps as I grow ever graceful in the practice of surrendering before what is too exhausting, or time-consuming, or beyond my physical or emotional reach, I will discover that there is *always* beauty, . . . and truth, . . . and goodness, just on the other side of changing attitude.

Soliloquy

I keenly remember
what it felt like
to stroke with my palm
and the soft undersides of my fingers
the curve of a woman's neck.
I would let the gravity of her body
coax my hand to her throat
where my thumb would slip
past her stretched larynx
and rest on firm muscles.

There is a beauty
uniquely a woman's body.
The beauty of a Winter's sunset
also unique
and with its own hyperboles
is not greater
or less
than the touch of fine down
on a woman's cheek.
I watch the sun
between light showers
flash gold on the evergreens;
I silently study the delicate variations
in the blue of a Stellar's Jay
busy at the feeder;
I wash my face in the warmth and sweetness

of Muphin's hairy belly. . . .
Beauty abounds
and feeds my senses.

And sometimes
invited by a curl of smoke
I remember that other beauty:
the route along her jaw
the edges of an upper lip
just beneath the nose
the odors of skin and breath
intermingling.

For much of my life
this passionate mindfulness
of another woman's body
has been my theology.
Now, I worship in soil of my own
study my aging hands
float my fingers over raised veins.
I follow the well-developed lines
of my arm muscles
examine my dappled skin
peer through its thinning sheen
into the exquisite blue lace at my wrists
push the membrane into a sea of wrinkles.

My appetite for beauty has not diminished
nor has my satiety.
I merely note
that the delicacies in my nearest pasture
are fare for calm
solitudinal
grazing.

Gates to Live By

There are many ways to reckon the past twenty years of *Fly Away Home*. First there were the two of us here, then four for a few years, then – and still – the original two of us again. The garden grew from modest plantings for Summer and Autumn dinners, to a 10,000 square-foot fenced "vegetable park" which feeds us year-round, and flowers abound on a hillside once a briar patch. History is told by the increasing number of holes in the roof of the venerable old barn, where wind has sucked away many of the shingles, dark and brittle with age, and by the buckling of one of the barn walls where a floor beam at last rotted through, a beam no doubt harvested from the nearby forest, like all the wood in this relic. The forest itself tells a tale, as some vistas have been cut off by the growing tops of evergreens, and others opened as those same trees lose their lower branches, inviting me to gaze deep into the forest, and beyond. Recently I discovered that the sunset now glows full-orbed through the self-thinning grove just west of my house.

I read history in the changes, the making-new, the letting-go, the deaths of animal companions, the arrival of new ones . . . the openings and closings of the chapters of my country life. Like the openings and closings of gates, each change is a passageway from the past to the future.

When Bethroot and I came to explore this hill in March of 1976, there was no gate at the entrance to the dirt road which snaked through a neighbor's ridge of timber for over a mile, ascending from the blacktop county road up to just within the boundary of what would become our home. A gate was the last thing on my mind as I leapt onto this lap, and knew I was truly coming *home*, knew I was beginning a love with this earth to hold and carry me for the rest of my life.

Actually, there wasn't much need for a gate as a deterrent to intruders, given that the road itself was nearly impassable. The deep ruts in the clay, softened by the late Winter rains, were testament to Big Blue's dogged ability to make it up the steep muddy road, manageable by neither of our cars.

A couple months and over a thousand dollars later, the road had been changed from an unwelcoming gauntlet of ruts, mud, and potholes to a fairly driveable dirt and gravel run. Word must have gotten out to the townspeople fifteen miles away that there were new residents at the "old Pate place," and that we had fixed the road. As Spring warmed into Summer many an evening's sunset was interrupted by a car suddenly appearing at the "stable" (where the horsepower is parked: we did not want a "parking lot" in the country). The stories from the men behind the wheel varied from having gotten lost, to simply wanting to have a look at the place where they had visited the Pate family some decades earlier, or used as a trysting place when the land had been deserted for a few years in the late sixties. I suspect all of them were curious about these two apparently husbandless women, who proposed to make a go of it on this isolated hilltop.

Wanting solitude and a home separated from, and uninterrupted by, the men's world as much as possible, we decided to erect some kind of gate down at the bottom of the road, with a No Trespassing sign, and a combination lock attached. That first barrier to unwanted visitors was a heavy thick sisal rope stretched between two yew posts, all items we found among the welcome materials left by the former owners. We labored mightily to sink those eight-foot posts two feet deep into the rocky ground, our first feat with a pickax and the posthole digger. (The extensive garden fence came some years later.)

Bethroot and I were still new at doing big work projects together. Two Springs before, in her rented backyard in the city, we had put in a small garden, though I knew next to nothing about gardening back then. When we came to this land we were faced with work to do which made mockery of our previously assumed limits. We learned how to perch safely on high ladders to work on the unfinished house, fix leaks in the mile-long waterline, install additional pipe for the propane system . . . and wield a post-hole digger.

A few months later the rope was replaced by a more sturdy heavy metal link chain, donated by the neighbor who was interested in protecting his timber from firewood-seeking poachers. We installed the lock and gave the combination to our new dyke friends in the area, and included it on the maps we sent out to old lovers and city-friends, and other women who came from afar to befriend and celebrate our country home.

So, first the rope, then the chain, were about shutting out energy we did not want coming up the road. The sign and the lock announced this was not a public road, not a route for Sunday drives, that we wanted privacy and were not available for unsolicited visitors. And such interruptions did stop, except for when the Pate sisters walked up the road one Summer day to courteously ask to say hello to their childhood's home. Their reckoning of the passing of time was by the spreading growth of the forest; they were amazed at how tall the evergreens had grown, how thickly they and the sinewy madrones hugged the new round house. I could almost see the land in its former visage from their descriptions, and was glad these women understood the chain on the road had some welcome in its links.

But that chain-gate was clumsy to deal with when time came for the day-long trips to town for supplies. Eventually, when we each had jobs which took us away from home two to three days a week, struggling with the chain became a downright nuisance, one we bore with much frustration.

When Bonnie and Izetta moved in, after we had been here about three years, there were even more goings and comings, as well as more energy available to make some improvements. Some friends living at Rainbow's Other End, a sisterland about an hour away, had two old slatted wooden panels built originally to raise the side-height of truckbeds, and offered them to us as possible gates. Now this was a step up! Swinging gates! No more hauling the heavy chain out of the way or straining to pull it taut enough to get the lock on it again. Unfortunately, the yew posts were too close together to accommodate the span of the wooden panels; we'd have to remove them. Getting those posts out was even harder than installing them had been. Bethroot and I had done a good job of pounding rocks down into the holes around the posts; we fit them firmly around a nubbin of a branch sticking out on the side of one of the posts, which then defied extraction. The four of us took turns with the digging and pulling, and grunting. That back-breaking removal marked the beginning of my really under-standing that nothing is permanent, even though it is necessary to build as though it were.

We used fir timbers treated with crankcase oil for the new posts, taller and thicker than the yew, placed about eighteen feet apart, one on each side of the road. With strap hinges, we hung the panels, which I had braced with diagonal boards, between the posts. Izetta and I installed the latch: a heavy-duty metal bar on the longer of the two gates, designed to slip through a similar metal hoop on the shorter one, which would remain stationary, except when the huge propane delivery truck came through once a year. Near the latch we wrapped a short length of metal chain from one gate to the other, and on that placed the combination lock. Then we painted both gates and posts dark green, to protect the wood from weathering as well as give an overall appearance of beauty and care. The finishing touches were two round orange reflectors on the county road side, insurance against anybody driving into the possibly unseen gates on a dark rainy Oregon night.

This was one of the first tasks Izetta and I shared, and it was one of those scenes where I figured I knew more than she did about how to do such things as hang a gate and install a latch. Between my presumptuousness and her short temper, we added a bit of tension to the job. But we worked resolutely together to improve the opening to our home, despite the mis-match we sometimes were. We built our relationship as Bethroot and I had put in those original posts: digging into the packed resistance of our individual histories and choices, pushing past the obstacles of our sometimes-conflicting expectations, defying the hardness, bravely and determinedly choosing our loving despite rock-bottom differences.

That wooden panel gate went on to serve this land for fifteen years, long after both Izetta and Bonnie had moved away. It survived both those loverships, and other openings and closings of the heart. Back to just the two of us, Bethroot and I each licked our wounds, some of which we caused each other. We worked the land, planted and reaped in abundance, and celebrated the changing of the seasons with the friends and strangers who passed through our gate, leaving behind the noise and harshness of the world beyond. I earned my reputation as a recluse in earnest, learning to love my singularity, and reserving my heart for the land and my animal family.

Over time the longer gate sagged, no longer restrained by the diagonal bracing; the paint peeled, the wooden slats cracked and bent under the stress, and began to rot. The latch bar no longer slid easily through the hoop, requiring a lifting of the gate to open and close it, an increasingly annoying chore. Last Summer I figured the gate was nearing her end, though I hoped she'd last yet another year.

Come Autumn someone else apparently decided we needed a new gate, for one day, when I was away helping a friend with a construction project, Bethroot discovered that the long gate had been smashed. Pieces of the horizontal slats lay splintered on the road, the space between the verticals gaping and tongued with broken boards. Bethroot used some scrap pieces of wood and a portable power drill to make as good a temporary repair as she could, but these were bandaids and a new gate was in order.

Pushed to take on the project I had wanted to delay, I found I welcomed it. Yes, it was time for something new at the entrance to this home, something that would announce change. Time to declare the gate erected by four was worn out, time for me to celebrate my success at nurturing a satisfying wholeness in my single life, my freedom from the pain of the past.

We were almost ready to buy a metal gate from the Farm Co-op, but I noticed, on another country road, a gate made from poles, simple and attractive. So I designed something similar for what we needed to span the twelve feet between the fir post and the intact and strong shorter gate. I selected poles from the forest, young trees who had abandoned their quest for sunlight beneath the tall canopy and fallen to the ground, still solid enough to be transformed into the members of a gate. Bethroot stripped most of the poles and I set to the carpentry, working on flat ground at the stable. For the better part of a week I had a good time constructing this gate, working slowly and carefully to make it as beautiful as my skills, twenty years in the honing, could produce. Working with handtools, I cut and chiseled thirty lap-joints, fine-tuned to fit together snugly, then assembled most of the posts to the rails with long nails, predrilling holes for them to make sure the poles would not split. I drilled holes for the bolts I'd use to hold the fifteen-foot diagonal in place, the strengthening hypotenuse that would give a sense of triangularity to an essentially horizontal gate.

Because of the length and height of the design, it was not possible to completely assemble the gate at the stable, so sections of it had to be laid on Big Blue's bed and driven to the site. There I finished the assembly, while Bethroot cut back the blackberries spilling down the bank beside the road, clogging the ditch and trailing into the gateway.

Bethroot and I hung the gate together, which involved taking what was left of the old gate off its strap hinges, reclaiming them and a few of their bolts for the new gate. I had to drill new holes in the still-solid fir timber in order to relocate the hook part of the hinges. Getting it just right meant we had to lift the heavy gate into and out of position several times before it swung with ease.

I am proud of what I made, loved seeing it come into being, loved making something even more beautiful than what was there before. This one is made entirely out of poles from the land, with no dimensional lumber involved; its parts are round and look like the trees they are. And I love the long diagonal brace which is a part of the gate itself, rather than adding on a wire cable for a brace, like the old one had (eventually bending the gate). That diagonal had inspired me to add more diagonals, making more triangles. The end effect is the space above the horizontal rails is a stylized flying creature that looks most like a butterfly to me. I elongated one of the shorter diagonals to effect a head, giving just the right amount of suggestion of a being, a flying being, a perfect welcome to *Fly Away Home.*

I have made many gates on this land: three for the garden, four for the fence around my house, now this one for the road. With this last one I entered a new world of gates, with design and creativity and beauty. The prior gates, more functional than aesthetic, are quite fine, and perfect for the work they do. But this one lifts me, and makes me fly, most every time I open and close it.

Recently I returned from a visit up north with my former mate and her partner. It had been over five years since I had last seen Izetta, and I knew Ellen only slightly a long time ago. I was ready to be with them, to give my blessing to their loving in their presence, to give myself the certain knowing of my healing. It was a successful journey, with gifts of understanding and compassion, playfulness and song. Home again, I opened the gate, then sat a few moments in the car, admiring this invitation at the bottom of our road. As I drove through the gateway, flanked by a yellow profusion of scotch broom, I felt myself moving through the story of my life, a story in part about opening and closing, opening and closing, like the gates that have stood sentinel to the road *Home.*

True Adventures

I pondered a book reviewer's opinion that it is necessary to leave home in order to have an adventure, and decided if by "adventure" is simply meant an experience out-of-the-ordinary, then I'd say I do not have to go away in order to have one, though I may have to pay deeper attention to where I am. Like when I looked up from the book I was reading over a mid-Spring breakfast to be surprised by the rare appearance of an Evening Grosbeak, vying with the much smaller Goldfinches for the sunflower seeds in the hanging feeder. Between them they wore several shades of bright yellow, splashed with the Finch's black cap, both with their black and white wing bars, coloration I associate with the tropics.

Another rarity greeted me one morning as I watered the flower boxes which outline the deck around my round house. A motion outside the fence at the far end of the vegetable garden caught my eye. I stopped my watering and spied a very large tannish-brown animal sauntering through the tall grass, soon out of my sight. I figured the little nasturtium seedlings could wait while I fetched my binoculars and headed on out the lane for a better look. The animal was facing away from me when I got just past the intervening grove of evergreens. Its rather huge rump suggested perhaps a neighbor's horse was on the loose and wandered the whole way up our hill, looking for greener pastures. I had a good close-up view with the binocs when said critter lobbed her – his? – head around her shoulders to stare back at me. I would have been delighted to thus meet a horse face-to-face, but this was no horse! I was making the brief acquaintance of a wild Elk. Brief, because when she took me in she promptly eased out of my view, and had disappeared into the forest by the time I got further out the lane. I've lived on this hill for twenty years and I had never seen an Elk here, and never knew they were easily as big as a full-size horse. It was like I had been on a twenty-year adventure whose time had come.

Yet another adventure came when Bethroot and I took action against the serious competition we'd been having in the strawberry beds for the past two years. We had tried covering the three beds with plastic tarps at night, which was a hassle, and wasn't effective enough anyway. And somebody was digging in the vegetable beds at night, perhaps the same person. We suspected a raccoon. So this year we bought a big trap, the kind which catches the critter alive in a cage. In early June, just when a few strawberries took on a pink blush, I baited the trap-cage with some store-bought big red succulent specimens, and placed it on the path between the beds, hoping to catch whoever might threaten to steal the promising-looking harvest. First thing the next morning I could see from my deck that the door had been sprung, and sure enough there was something sizable pacing inside. Still in my slippers, I rushed down for a closer look, and found, not a Ringtail at all, but a Gray Fox! Normally a rodent-hunting carnivore whose presence near the garden I might be grateful for, this fox apparently had a taste for juicy strawberries, though her angry snarl testified the berries had not been worth her hours of confinement.

I got some breakfast in me, and fed the cats and hens, before Muphin and I trudged up the hill to Bethroot's house. When I awakened her and announced a fox was in the trap, Bethroot was amazed and excited. She had mourned the two fox kits she had seen dead on the county road in recent months, so was grateful for this opportunity to be up close to a live one. While she dressed, I returned to the house with Muphin, filled her bowl with home-made kibble, and explained that the wild creature down in the garden was someone Bethroot and I needed to handle without her curious, and likely hostile, company.

The Gray Fox half-barked, half-growled as we covered the trap with a cloth, hoping if she saw less, she'd have less to be nervous about as we lugged the bulky cage and its cargo out of the garden and up to the lane, to Bethroot's station wagon. We drove down our hill, then east on the county road, and up the mountain to Red Top Spring. We carried the cage to a little clearing in the forest, removed the cloth, and I slowly turned the wire box on its side, then its top, the fox preoccupied with adjusting herself accordingly. The door was thus released and fell open, and our would-be strawberry thief fled into the forest. Bethroot and I sang a blessing to her, wished her well in her new home.

I reset the trap, just in case there might be yet other critters interested in the berries, and two mornings later, voilá, another Gray Fox! This one was a little smaller and darker, so we knew the first had not simply come back. So off we went again on an early morning trip up mountain. In the ensuing weeks there were no more captives, except for the big Robin, who tripped the lever when hopping toward the bait intended for a less common thief.

Grosbeaks, Elk, Gray Foxes: extraordinary fare in the day-in and day-out simplicity of my life. But the ordinary is no slouch, for that matter. In late May I watched quite ordinary little brown Wrens making a nest in a corner under the eave of my house. Actually, the initial nest-builder was trying out several corners, depositing twigs as though to start construction, then moving on to yet another corner of the twelve-sided house. The place finally chosen was the one between the cold frame and the row of deck chairs, about six feet above a potted blue lobelia I had set on a short table. For many hours each day one-by-one they brought twigs and fitted them together in the small recess between the overhanging rafters. I often watched out the window, and sometimes from a chair on the deck at a respectful distance. They knew I was watching, would look at me from their perch on a peripheral flower box or the lobelia table, and hesitate to go to the nest. Sometimes they'd go on up, and I felt known and trusted; other times they flew off with the twigs still in their beaks, and I understood I was just a bit too close. I assumed I'd never see the interior of this diminutive maternity ward, never feel the soft lining of chicken-down or dog hair I imagined within. The adventure was that these tiny birds, with a song big enough to fill the flower garden around my house, chose a part of my home as theirs.

One memorable day, the first of June, I spent a mellow afternoon communing with bright orange poppies in full bloom, the red climbing rose parading on the henhouse wall, the last of the irises waving their purple flags behind the pink snapdragons in the Wildbed, and on and on around the flower beds, paying my heartful respect to an assemblage of relatives. As yet I was not absolutely certain there was more than one Wren. I had seen them often, but actually never more than one at a time. I sat here and there among the beds all afternoon, and listened to the magnificent song of one Wren perched on the fence post while, yes, another flew to the nest-in-process, and yet another skitted around under the house and among the leafed-out wisteria branches. So then I knew a mating pair was likely.

As the weeks went on, it seemed the nest was occupied more frequently, and the songster of the pair spent more time on the fence post, outdoing even the volume of the fussy Stellar's Jays with his loud refrain. Smaller than the Purple Finches, and even the Goldfinches, this little brown bird with the mottled white chest could easily get my attention while I was busy with tasks indoors, or down in the vegetable garden. I could almost always find him atop the garden post, or on the adjacent fencing. Watching as much as I did, I felt these birds, as well as the flocks of Finches and Jays at the feeder, were a melodious, colorful part of my most intimate family.

Then I was gone for a week, to a women-writers' workshop, where I loved working among lots of other writers, inspired by good teachers. I did miss Muphin, and mused about the birds at the feeders, and the Wrens, all of whom eventually found their way into the material I wrote. When I returned home on a Friday, I had unpacking to do, a meeting to go to an hour's drive away the next day, and sleep to catch up on. I almost immediately watered the deck boxes, happy to see how much the nasturtiums had grown, but it wasn't until Monday that I went out to look up at the nest, hoping to see some activity. Somewhere between conscious thought and a mental twilight I had been missing the song of the Wren, though it took me three days to investigate.

I stood just a couple feet away from the house wall, the nest about three feet above my head, and soon became mesmerized by a very very odd scene: one of the Wrens on the outside of the nest, unmoving, her legs attached to the nest, her feathers mussed. I just stood there. Time stopped. I wanted to see her move, I longed for this scene to be replaced by something else, something to make my hanging jaw close with a smile, with relief. She did not move, not a foot or a wing, not a feather. I had to get closer, made myself turn and walk a pie section's worth of the deck to where the wooden step ladder stood in its place, carried the ladder to beneath the nest and set it up, climbed so that my head was only a few inches below the nest. And still the little Wren did not move. Nor would she ever.

I gently pulled the Wren off the side of the nest and lifted her into my hand. Wrapped around one foot was a single strand of white filament from a plastic feed sack, like the ones the hens' food comes in. The strand uncurled a few inches, then disappeared inside the nest. I pulled on it, at first tentatively, which had little effect, then tugged in earnest to extricate a wad of the plastic, woven into the lining of the nest. Standing there on the ladder, the Wren in my palm, the white strands trailing, I was swept into another dimension, now seeing the little bird taking off from the edge of her nest, only to be violently jerked back by the unsuspected shackle on her leg. I saw her grab the side of the nest, then try again, and again, and again. . . . I heard her fluttering struggle, felt her panic. Again a leap, again the jerk. Did her leg break that first time, or after repeated thrusts? Did she hang there for days and die of starvation, or did she die quickly from a broken heart?

The pain, the struggle, the despair pulsed through my body. The shock erupted in a raging howl. I pounded my fist on the top of the ladder; sobbing as deep and loud as I have ever known boiled from my belly and chest. Muphin lay nearby, quiet and watchful, as I stood on the ladder wailing, tears washing my cheeks, my nose dripping. I held onto the ladder and sobbed until my legs were too weak to support me. The Wren and her fetter still in my hand, I let myself down the ladder and eased into a deck chair, where my sobbing transformed from rage at the unjust universe, into an overwhelming sense of loss.

The Finches were busy at the feeders when my bawling had softened to a moaning cry. But there was no live Wren singing atop the fence post, no sight of the mate of the dead bird in my hand. The horrible thought suddenly came to me that maybe there were baby birds in the nest. I did not know how to care for hatchlings, having always left this work to the mama hens. When I felt steady on my feet again I laid the body beside the lobelia and climbed back up the ladder. Slowly I walked my fingers over the edge of the nest, then down into the twiggy cavity. To my relief there were no birds, only the thwarted promise of them: I carefully lifted out four little creamy-tan eggs, each about as big as my thumb nail.

There was no happy ending to this story. No miraculous resurrection, not even the reappearance of the widower with a new mate to sing for. I buried the Wren, with her sweet tiny eggs, beneath a new Rock Rose down near the fence line. My grief grew into resignation and acceptance. This, too, was an adventure, the kind that ends in tragedy. Mountain climbers are sometimes swallowed by an avalanche, voyagers drowned at sea. And the stay-at-home variety of adventure has death for its eventual and certain destination, as surely as does all of life. The Gray Foxes hunting up the mountain, the ambling Elk, the flocks I feed, . . . Muphin . . . and I, will each be pulled by a fatal strand toward our demise. For that ultimate adventure, I won't have to leave home either.

Sami Slate Died Today
August 27, 1996

I want to bury you
in a place you loved.

I could tuck you
into the skin
of my side and underarm
where you lay panting
one long Summer night
anxiously pregnant
with your last-born.
Or in the flesh of my thigh
where you reposed most mornings
a Buddha
while I meditated.
My pelvis would gladly hold you
recall your sleeping
curled on my mound
as I napped.
I could lay you
beneath the surface of my face
take our nuzzling bone-deep.
My chest wants
to cradle
and rock
the weight of you,
so slight in these last weeks,

your muted purr
resonating my ribbed refrain
in the minutes before you died.
I would give
the sinews of my palms
to the jet-black velvet of your fur
carry each nob of your spine
within my gnarled fingers.

But tomorrow
I will work the earth
to an opening
and cover you with soil
my body
a graveyard of memories.

The Winter of Binder Creek

Evenings are dark and long in this southern Oregon Winter. A long soak in a deep hot bath can be a pleasant way to pass some time, as well as cleansing. But the water pressure in our spring-fed gravity-flow system had been seriously low for several weeks, and I was getting mighty annoyed at how long it took to fill even a few inches of my old porcelain claw-foot tub, and with brownish water at that. Bethroot and I surmised the spring tank which feeds the waterline must be full of silt, though we had cleaned it in October. Maybe there were some plug-ups in the pipe line, barely letting water through. While we can always get drinking water by the jug-fulls from the little spring beyond my Poogoda, on the way to the East Side, that emergency method wears thin after a while, suffices for only the minimum of needs, and it's a long haul to Bethroot's house further up the hill. She had pulled on me earlier in the new year to go up to deal with this problem with her, but my energy and the weather did not coalesce until this week's late January sunny respite from the rain.

In addition to October's regular seasonal attention to the tank, we had already exhausted ourselves on several occasions with extra work caused by Autumn's heavy rains. In early November a tall fir adjacent to the road, its moorings softened by weeks of nearly incessant drenchers, toppled down the steep east bank and took a chunk of the edge of the road with it. That repair required hauling huge rocks from elsewhere along the road, and stuffing them into the hole where the tree's roots had been, a hole which potentially undermined the road. Then there were the three Blue-loads of gravel we fetched and spread, and packed with our feet, where the road surface had gotten soft; and the days we labored to cut back the infant trees and brush that had grown in some places to clog access to the ditch, causing damaging flooding of the road.

In the darkness of one late rainy evening Bethroot returned home from town to find bunch grass grown so tall and dense in and around the ditch near the gate that it lay a thick carpet in the water's path, and completely thwarted the ditch's job. The water had jumped the channel and was pouring onto the road, forcing her to stand in rushing water up to her ankles as she opened and closed the gate. She was already tired from the fine-tuning of gravel on the first steep section she had done alone in the morning, so that night, barely in the beam of her station wagon's headlights, I fiercely hacked with a hoe at the thick resistance until the water returned to its proper place.

I was a bit miffed as I forced my tired arms to wield the hoe to clear about fifty feet of ditch, having warned some weeks before that this grass would cause serious difficulty if the ditch got too full with run-off. But Bethroot had other priorities, and we often got caught in our pattern of disagreeing about how to do what, and where, each of us convinced we had the better solution to whatever problem we faced together. If we had been more aligned, she would not have gotten wet feet, and I would not have been out there struggling with grass and water in the dark.

Too, if I had been willing to bestir myself earlier to tend the tank, Bethroot would not have had to haul so many gallons up the hill, and I would have been having my content of baths. While I was not looking forward to another labor-intensive scene which might give rise to argument, it was clearly time to get back up to the spring tank. So yesterday we loaded up the tools and equipment needed, and our lunches, including some biscuits for Muphin, and drove up White Rock Road into BLM country.

The trees siding the dirt and gravel logging road have grown thick and tall in these more than twenty years, covering the view toward our forty acres. Where once I stood at a bend in the road and called a blessing across the ravine to the land we wanted, but were told we could not have, where I hooted a lovespell and was answered by the resident rooster, where once we could see the sun shining on Big Blue and reflecting off the stovepipe on the roof of what was to become our common house for seventeen years, now it would be impossible to spy our homestead beyond the curtain of evergreens.

After an ascent of about two miles from the county road, we parked the car on the shoulder, at the spot where we could begin the descent to the draw of Binder Creek. Muphin was eager for the outing, started down the path as soon as she saw we were loaded with our packs and would be following. Over the years, we have slowly clipped out a trail down to the site of this rather primitive source of all the water servicing our two houses, the trailer and gatehouse, our large vegetable garden, my many flower beds, and the henhouse. The steep slope from the road requires walking sideways for about fifteen feet, fending off a gauntlet of healthy poison oak, now leafless and grey-stemmed in its Winter visage. We have marked, with bright fuchsia logger's ribbon, the difficult route as it threads through brush and evergreens, winds around decaying logs, then comes out onto the old clear-cut which long predates our appearance here, and by the looks of the haphazard return growth, predates any program of planned reforestation, or else is a terrible testament to its failure. The way down to the spring, although no more than a few hundred feet, takes determination and care, holding on to a handy branch of young madrone here and there, with a sit-down slide on your rump in one place, climbing over a felled, then neglected, log in another.

Muphin's enthusiasm led the way, and I envied her easy four-legged footing as I picked my way down the rain-loosened forest floor and negotiated the logs. There is a discernible edge to the swath of timber left standing adjacent to the road, a demarcation I have always enjoyed for its opening of the view of the draw, though over time the scattered maples, madrones, and a few conifers have grown to shorten the view, as well as choke tiny Binder Creek feeding the spring. Where the path emerges from the dark thickness, a long sun-paled strip of ribbon gestures its guidance from a low branch. When we arrived at that ribbon yesterday, it had taken on the specter of a flag for special caution: long cracks lay across the face of the hill, the soil ripped apart like a badly worn piece of cloth. As we detoured around them, we came upon a broad expanse of the hillside which had slumped several feet, making a muddy fissure in the terrain. It looked like an earthquake had rumbled through, though we knew this was the work of this season's flooding rains, saturating soil never meant to lose its restraining forest. Another wide detour, and then the awesome sight of what that slump merely echoed: where there had been wild honeysuckle, red currant, tall bear grass, the little white tufts of pearly everlasting . . . where orange tiger lilies had waved us by on a late Spring's tank-tending mission, there was now a raw, barren, voluminous mass of oozing light-brown clay, obliterating our path and defying our passage.

This Winter has been the wettest in my memory. In truth, I have mostly enjoyed the weeks and weeks of rain which have given me permission to stay indoors more than usual, cozy with my knitting, reading, writing, and with the warm fuzzy company of Muphin and the two cats – aged Lillith One and her much bigger daughter Keaton. Of course the storms have demanded continued vigilance on the road, and Bethroot and I have taken care of each other by alternately taking care of the road, making trips with a hoe when either has seen the need to keep the ditches open, the water running where it does no harm. I am not one to listen much to the radio, do not have a TV, subscribe to no newspaper, but Bethroot keeps informed of the world's goings-on, and friends bring their tales of the sinkhole forcing closure of the Interstate for a couple weeks, massive lethal slides around the county, the destructive flood in Ashland further south. I have been especially grateful this season that Bethroot and I, over two decades ago, persevered in our passion for this land sitting on a hilltop, high above the present torrent of South Myrtle Creek. The occasional inconvenience of not having a telephone or AC electricity is more than matched by our independence from utility companies whose services have been interrupted by the floods. My composting privy, kerosene lamps and DC photoelectric system, propane-run refrigerator and cookstove, and my solar-and-woodstove water-heating system are unaffected by the weather which has sometimes temporarily stolen the security and comfort from some of my town-dwelling friends' lives. I had gotten to feeling a bit smug in my off-the-grid shangri-la.

The hike to the spring tank was humbling.

Muphin would have sprinted across the sloping field of mud, her fifteen pounds easily held afloat, but Bethroot and I knew better than to try to descend what had become an avalanche of clay. We worked our way north of the slide, and carefully started downward again where the soil looked undisturbed and the earth felt firm enough to carry our weight. The pitch of the hill was much steeper than our vanished path, requiring a crab's gait, one well-placed sideways step at a time. A few feet above the narrow bed of Binder Creek we met a small patch of bare clay, and were amazed to find, not the almost invisible streamlet we knew well, but a true rushing small creek, the water tumbling through and under a tangled skein of debris left by the old logging, young trees bent and brooding over the turbulent water. A misplaced step and my foot was dangling in the ravel. Bethroot placed some twigs on the clay for a better footing while she waited patiently for me to extricate myself, then guided Muphin to follow me. Her little paws were a disadvantage in the puzzle of small branches; I caught her just before she would have slipped down into a wet woody maze. I made a mental note to bring some planks and make a bridge for all of us.

Once across the creek we could see the twenty or so feet downstream to the spring tank. As we maneuvered our way closer, the area surrounding it looked different from when we had last made this trek. Now there was more sky showing, and less open space on the ground around the one hundred gallon, thick plastic tank.

"Oh . . . my . . . ge-ahd," was all I could say, as Bethroot and I gaped at the scene, then in wonder at each other. The slide which had swallowed our path extended the whole way to the foot of the tank, splintered and knocked over trees, gouged at roots. A two-feet high mound of sodden clay had flowed over the draping excess of the sheet of black plastic covering the six-foot panel of galvanized metal roofing, which in turn protects the screen over the tank. The panel extends up over the metal half-drum shelter for the wooden trough, now corralling the loud run of Binder Creek to feed the tank. If the push of the slide had reached just four feet further north, our modest tap into the goddess's plenty would have been buried, perhaps even overturned and broken. The tan toe of the slide nudged just the edge of the tank.

Both Bethroot and I were struck by Nature's power and whim: she had come so close to destroying the head of the system on which we are dependent. True, she had created some serious problems for us: the pipe exiting from the tank, and its shut-off valve, lay beneath half a foot of water, covered by the plastic and its formidable weight of mud. In order to clean out the tank, we needed to close that valve, so as to not feed the stirred-up silt into the system, and risk adding to any plugs. The immediate job, of just getting to the valve, was rather overwhelming for the two of us. And it would take a crew to dig out and haul away all the bank of clay which partially dammed the creek, making a new foot-deep icy pool where the tank's drain valve was located, and where we'd have to stand to clean the tank.

Our homesteading, spring-tending predecessors had left a shovel with a welded metal handle at the site, a tool we have often used to clear the creek's silt and stony droppings from the various water-catchers the system has seen over the years. First there was the metal fifty-five gallon drum, installed on a slant at a knee-bend in the bed; then, when that drum's function was compromised by rusted-out holes grown to finger-size, we replaced it with a food-grade plastic one. Then last year, with the help of hard-working friends and three different trips with the equipment, we made a leap into the modern age with this bigger livestock-watering tank. This has proved a far more effective way of capturing the water, which fills and overflows the tank. Before this avalanche dramatically altered the terrain, the overflow then ran off into a tunnel in the bank, and continued on its way down the draw, to disappear underground again. Now the water stayed above-ground and accumulated around the tank before it followed its course.

The old shovel hung in a forked maple, which had grown from the green sapling we encountered the first time we investigated the spring tank in '76, to a grey thick-trunked stabilizer at the upstream end of the tank. In spite of the enormity of the task at hand, I grabbed the shovel and got busy. I had not planned on so severe a test of my new, hopefully waterproof, boots, as I stood ankle-deep in the water and began digging at the mass.

"I don't know that a more quickly-filling bathtub is worth all this effort," I wondered aloud. But the job would have to be done sooner or later, and we had struggled down the steep hill with the intent of accomplishing something, so we both set to work with good spirits and comradery. I repeatedly sank the shovel into the mud and we both lifted the sodden weight. Trouble was, there really was nowhere to throw it all to avoid adding to the unwanted dam, and piling it on the opposite bank would eventually result in a mini slide. The latter was the least immediately frustrating, so we hefted the heavy clay as high as we could onto the bank, and knocked the sticky clods from the shovel. But as we dug away at the foot of the mound, gravity simply pulled more mud into its place. After about a half hour of vigorous and frustrating shovelling, we both complained of tiring muscles and we were each getting cranky, especially when it became apparent we were not going to be able to get to that valve. It would take more than the two of us . . . it would take a bucket brigade.

In this life we make in tandem, Bethroot and I have sometimes discovered that giving up can be the best way through a problem. Throwing in the towel when we get at loggerheads about what repair the road needs most, or how to plan the garden, usually moves at least one of us to a new perspective, and the road turns out just right, the garden flourishes. This time we were both up against The Mother, and backed off with respect. I don't remember who of us suggested we might open the first clean-out valve in the line, just a hundred feet downhill. Then the silt would hopefully flow out that drain, at the juncture where the two-inch black plastic pipe from the tank adapts down to the one-inch of our "Black Snake Creek." With this plan in mind, we pulled the plastic sheeting back enough to make it possible to lift off the metal panel, and then removed the half-drum, trough and screen. The water subsequently flowed short of the tank, which turned out to be two-thirds filled with silt and tiny stones, to about a foot below the brim.

Bethroot waded into the flowing creek and disappeared into the thicket of brush, trees, and debris to go open the valve, while I started shovelling out the bulk. I was grunting with the labor when she had completed her task and returned, with an alarming description of trees uprooted, branches flung about, the route along the line inaccessible. She had needed to climb above it until the effects of the slide ended, just a few feet shy of the valve. Her cheeks were pink from the effort, her smile a gesture of good humor in the face of adversity bigger than both of us. "Well, that hundred feet of pipe just will never need repair!" she declared, turning resignation into a chuckle.

My sense of myself is that over the years I became the one who has kept us both going when the going has gotten rough, I the one to maintain a hearty readiness and positive outlook when the physical challenges of this life have pushed us to our limits. I looked now at Bethroot's smile, the clusters of wrinkles it sculpted around her bright eyes, and understood that somewhere along the way we had become again allies in spirit as well as deed.

It took a great deal of shovelling, then scooping with the two large plastic dippers, made from laundry soap containers, to empty the tank of all but a slight and acceptable film on the bottom. Because the ground sloped beneath the tank, the pooled creek was deeper there (my boots had passed their test), so the tank became buoyant as we emptied it.

"I feel like I am bailing out a canoe!" I laughed, as we awkwardly struggled to keep the tank from floating and bobbing, which would put dangerous pressure on the pipe attached to it. Bethroot leaned her weight on the one end and I braced a knee on the other, as I reached down inside to the stainless steel mesh box attached to the outlet from the tank. I gently removed its fine-screen cover to reveal yet finer silt almost filling the box, and clogging the entrance to the pipe. At this point the dominant feeling was amazed gratitude. All that silt usurping precious space in the tank and choking the outlet, and yet we still had water down below. Perhaps not enough to satisfactorily fill a tub, or guarantee Bethroot's supply, but a steady flow nonetheless. In the past, when the collector was the slanted drum, we would have had no water at all, its small screen easily caked and blocked by the debris borne by the Winter-swollen creek. Bethroot and I were both proud of the improvement we had researched and invented, of the time spent working out every conceivable flaw, despite the present necessity of all the exhausting digging and bailing.

Using my rubber-gloved hands to rake out the box, I then pushed a length of sturdy wire into the pipe, loosening the clog, and counted on the thick silt finding its way to that open valve a hundred feet away. I re-secured the fine screen and the band which holds it in place, then we lifted the big screen onto the tank and replaced the trough. The tank filled with amazing speed, the flow of water obviously well in excess of the six or so gallons a minute we once measured.

During all this time Muphin had lain nearby, above-water, just out of the way of our work. She was unusually patient, spoke no whimpering boredom with her idleness. I guessed she understood the seriousness of our job, found enough entertainment in the odors of the forest. When we got all the coverings back in place, and hoisted our packs for the trek down the pipe, she quickly jumped into line between Bethroot and me with the excitement of a walk in the woods. A little too quickly, for Bethroot almost landed on her when she lost her balance for a moment and fell backwards on a log she had just climbed over.

"No! No! Don't sit down!" I shouted, as I grabbed Muphin out of the way.

"I am not sitting, I'm falling!" Bethroot shouted back. We were tired by then, and feeling the downside of awe, so the comical aspect of this scene was welcome, sending us both briefly into giggles.

Since the path along the waterline had been claimed by the slide's debris, I followed Bethroot on the higher route to the first clean-out valve. Neither of us said much as we made our way down to the pipe. I supposed she was as anxious as I was about whether we would find the hoped-for fountain of water spewing from the open valve. To our great disappointment, the only sound of water running was coming, not from our pipe, but from the creek well below it, deeper in the draw.

Sometimes I find defeat unacceptable, and plunge toward solution in spite of the face of things. I picked up that flexible two-inch pipe and shook it, willing the silt and stones to thin themselves, willing the water through. Heavy dark-brown liquid gurgled from the valve, then stopped. More shaking, more liquid. Bethroot joined the effort at a slight dip in the pipe ten or so feet above me, and between the two of us we shook the pipe clean. What a satisfying pleasure it was to watch the steady strong flow of clear spring water pummel the slick base of a cedar a good seven feet away.

We had a plan then: one of us would go on ahead to the next valve, and hoot as loud as she could when she reached and opened it. The other would stay behind and close the upper valve when she heard the hoot, then come down the line shaking the pipe wherever it lay yet uncovered by the decades' slow burial from rotting leaves and fallen branches on the forest floor. We traded jobs as we went, each, including Muphin, getting in some rest and lunch as we trudged our way through the next eight valves, and in this way gradually flushed the entire line, at long last emerging from the forest just above Bethroot's house.

We were all exhausted and wet from the day's adventure, and it was nearly suppertime, but we still had Bethroot's car to retrieve. She stopped to change clothes, and Muphin and I continued down the hill to our house, where I got into some dry sweats while Muphin warmed herself by the woodstove, banked before we left in the morning. We met at the stable for the drive in my car back up White Rock Road. As I led the way back down the mountain again I noticed the top of another slide, one which had extended to the road and taken a bite out of the surface at the edge. I thought about those cracks we had come upon earlier in the day, and wondered what more changes in the scenery, and in our lives, the Winter rains might yet bring.

I had plenty of leftovers in the frig only needing to be reheated, so invited Bethroot to join me for supper and a soothing completion of our day. While she put the vegetable stew to warm on the stove, and added more greens to the salad, I mixed up a batch of biscuits. As we ate, we reflected on the day's work, and on the preponderance of change. Nothing lasts forever in this country life – not the repairs we make on the road or the garden fence, not the paths, the buildings, the lives of our beloved animals, or even the visions of what we each aim to create here. We are regularly pushed to reinvent the wheel, or else replace it with something better. Both in our late fifties now, with enough experience to know all crises pass and we'll survive them, including our bouts of reciprocal discontent, we appreciate our tandem partnership with the land, each thankful to the other for what she creates here.

That night my tub filled quickly and I gratefully soaked my aching back and sore feet in the hard-earned product of our labors. Muphin lay on the bathmat in the glow of candlelight, sleeping through my gentle serenade: "One bright morning, as we work together, gonna *Fly Away Home*."

Notes on Prior Publication

Some of the material included in this volume has been published before, though most in earlier versions now revised.

"Fly Away Home": *Womanspirit*, Spring 1977

"And the Last Shall be Phyrste" (originally titled "Phyrste"):
                     Common Lives/Lesbian Lives, January 1985

"Autumn": *Maize, a Lesbian Country Magazine*, Fall 1986

"January Felling": *Common Lives/Lesbian Lives*, Winter 1986

"Recycling": *Maize*, Summer 1990

"Visit/ Visitation": the anthology *Our Lives: Lesbian Personal Writings*, ed. by Frances Rooney, Second Story Press, 1991

"Gender Studies": *Maize*, Fall 1993

"Making Family": *Maize*, Winter 1994

"Weeding at Dawn": *Maize*, Spring 1994

"Scrap": *Maize,* Fall 1994

"Arborescent": *Maize*, Spring 1995

"Altaring": *Maize*, Summer 1995

"Daring Acquiescence": *Maize*, Winter 1995

"Egg Song": *Maize*, Summer 1996

"Barometric": *Maize*, Fall 1996

"Gates to Live By": *Maize*, Spring 1997

"True Adventures": *Maize*, Fall 1997

About the Author

Hawk Madrone (a chosen name) was born in 1939 in Hanover, a small working-class town in south central Pennsylvania. She overcame the massiveness of Penn State University to earn a Master's degree in Philosophy. Thirteen years and two careers later (philosophy professor and auto mechanic), she began her life on the remote womensland that she and her land partner would call *Fly Away Home*, where she has lived for nearly a quarter century. Her home is her sanctuary, a women-only hilltop in southern Oregon, where there is music, food, spiritual ritual . . . the magic of strong bodies and hearts. With her animal companions always nearby, she is a woodworker, gardener, photographer, baker, embroiderer, woodswoman, writer . . . who intends Tai Chi as a way of life.

Madrone began being called by the second half of her name when she turned 45, having decided it was time to focus more on rooting rather than flying. With that rooting came a serious commitment to writing about her life on the land, the wisdom given to her by trees, animals, lovings and leavings, hard work, the weather . . . adventure.

Her poetry and prose have been published in *Womanspirit; Common Lives/Lesbian Lives; We 'Moon: Gaia Rhythms for Women; Maize: A Lesbian Country Magazine; Manzanita Quarterly;* and in the anthologies *Our Lives: Lesbian Personal Writings; The Poetry of Sex; The Wild Good;* and *An Intricate Weave.* In addition, she has self-published and marketed *Creation Story,* a Lesbian Feminist alternative to *Genesis.*